Paintings
2018-2020

Bob Diercksmeier

Cover art Copyright ©2020 Bob Diercksmeier
All images and text Copyright ©2020 Bob Diercksmeier
All rights reserved.

See more of my work at bdabstracts.com

For merchandise see cactusvibe.com

My other landscape work can be found at rjdfineart.com

For Amanda, Cy, and Elena

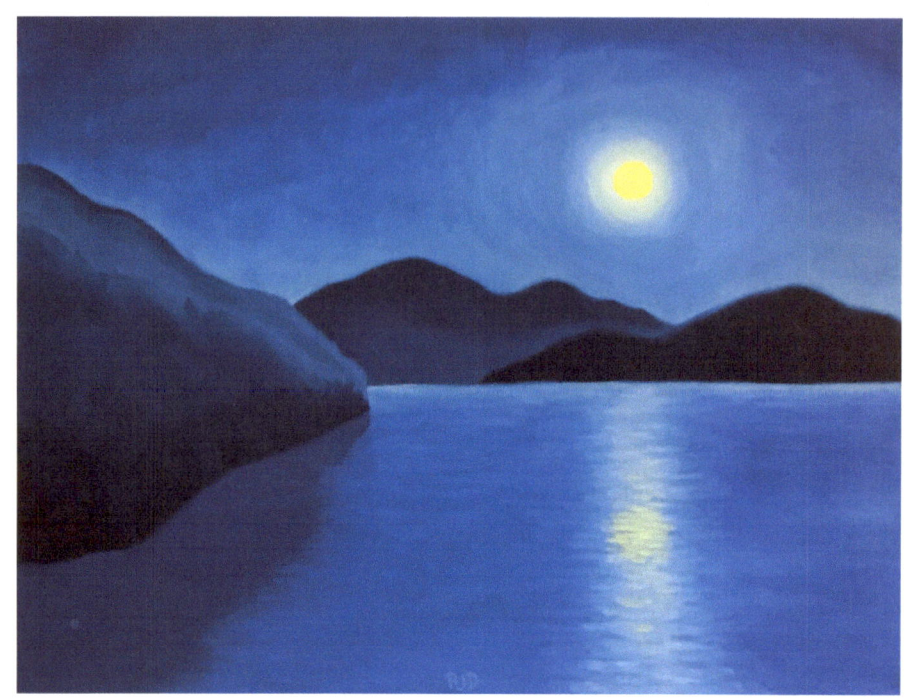

Saguaro Shimmer
2017, Oil on Canvas, 18 x 24 inches (45.72 x 60.96 cm)

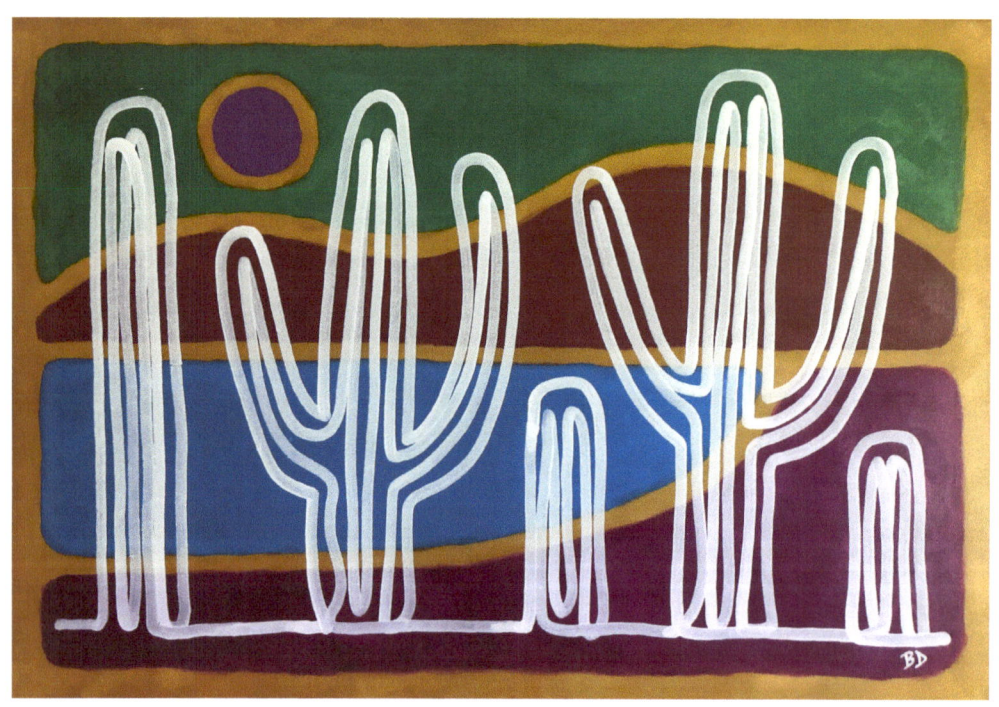

Saguaro Lake
2018, Acrylic on Canvas, 24 x 36 inches (60.96 x 91.44 cm)

A New Direction

A year or so after graduating from art school to become a freelance illustrator, I discovered the unique beauty of landscape painting. I was living in Connecticut at the time, and many accomplished landscape painters were living and working there whose works I would see in the galleries I'd visit. A few years later, I moved back to my home state of Arizona and rediscovered the desert landscape in which I had grown up. The Sonoran desert has both vibrant energy and a quiet mystery that combine to make it a unique place.

At the same time, I discovered the work of two incredible painters — Ed Mell and Gary Ernest Smith — who at the time were showing their work at the Overland Trail Gallery in Scottsdale. Upon seeing their work, a bell was rung deep within my artistic soul, and I knew that the future would see me painting my interpretations of the desert landscape. I had done some landscape work in Connecticut with east coast themes, and now I would focus my sights on the desert vistas around my home city of Phoenix.

Years passed, working as an illustrator, art director, and web designer, then marriage, kids, and family life, all good things. The landscape work was still part of the picture, happening here and there. In 2015 the fire reignited, and I begin painting again, initially in more abstracted landscape works, then more representational, although stylized (you can see this work at rjdfineart.com). My approach was reductive, dealing with broader pictorial issues and trying not to get caught up in the details. Plein air painting was also a necessity, creating work outdoors, straight from nature, to have a personal interaction with the subject, to experience natural color in person, directly with the naked eye. Even just sketching or doing color studies in the wild informed the work.

Color was always the focus, rooted in my study of Josef Albers' color theory at The University of Bridgeport in the mid-1980s. Color interaction has always been a central element in my work and remains so to this day. Transparent colors layered over one another, opaque color areas next to each other, opaque color with color showing through broken areas, all have different qualities and characteristics. The variety of ways colors react to each other in different situations has always interested me, and experimentation with new and different methods of color application would soon follow in a new body of work.

In the summer of 2018, I began some exploration in my sketchbook with a wandering line. That line naturally gravitated to landscape subjects — earth and mountain, sun, moon, and sky. Also entering the mix were the cacti that I would experience on my frequent hikes on the trails in and around Phoenix, four species in particular — the Saguaro, Prickly Pear, Barrel Cactus, and Organ Pipe. These are the four I see most frequently, so I have featured these as my subjects, my muses, if you will, in my work since that time.

The continuous line in my work came to represent the ongoing spirit of life that cacti maintain in the severe climate of the Sonoran desert. I began representing landscape elements with flat, organic forms. The ever-present element of color, from subtle earth tones to intense, vibrant hues, remained central to the work. My interpretation of line, form, and color — the three main elements of pictorial composition — was the combination of a continuous line, organic shapes, and subtle or vibrant pigment.

The work on the following pages represents the beginnings of my exploration of a more abstract approach to picture-making. This book features the paintings produced in the last two years — I have separate books that show drawings and prints made during the same period. You may see evolution as I started my journey down this new road of representation of subject and experimentation with medium and surface, both in service to a central goal — giving the viewer a sense of the magic and mystery of the desert environment and its marvelous cast of characters.

I hope you enjoy what you see.

Bob Diereksmeier
May 2020

The Paintings

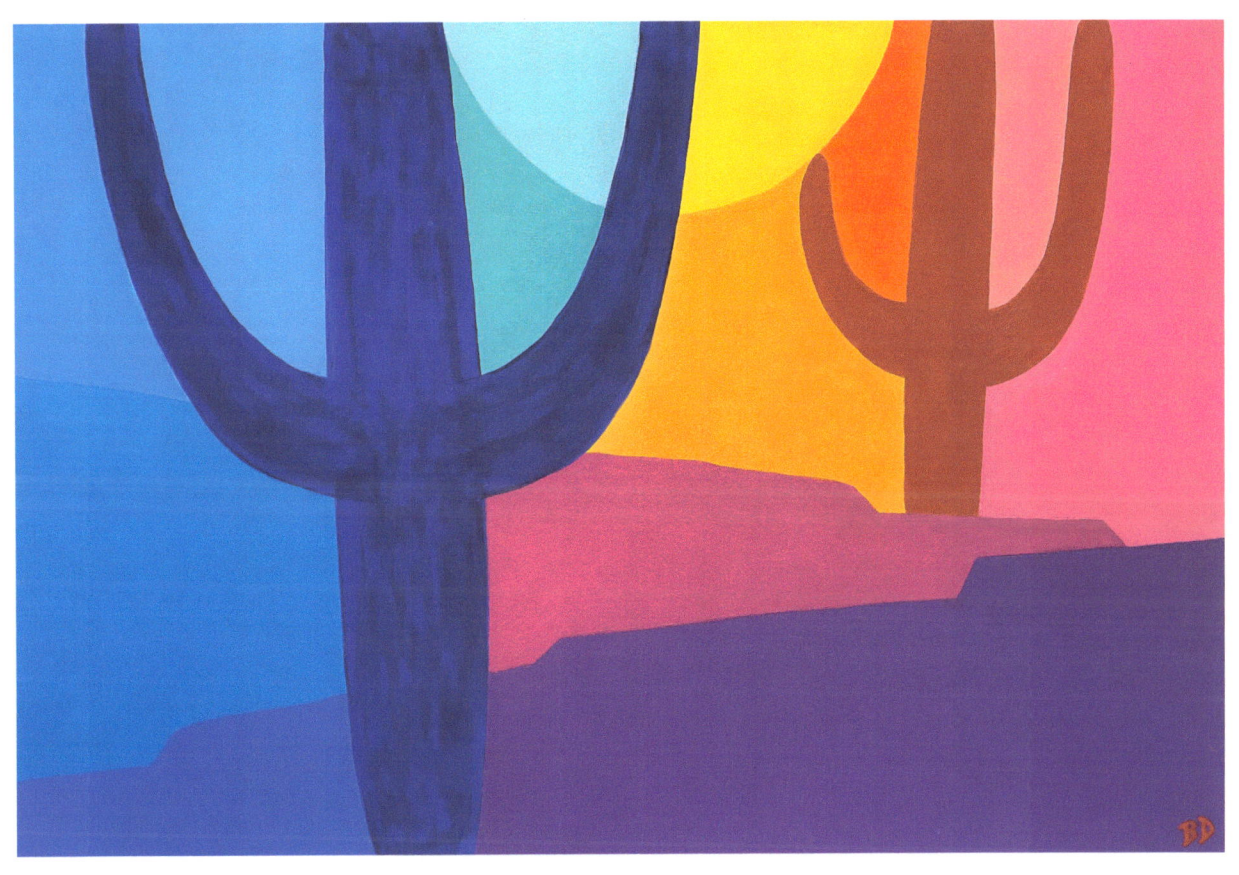

Saguaro Mosaic
2019, Acrylic on Canvas, 24 x 36 inches (60.96 x 91.44 cm)

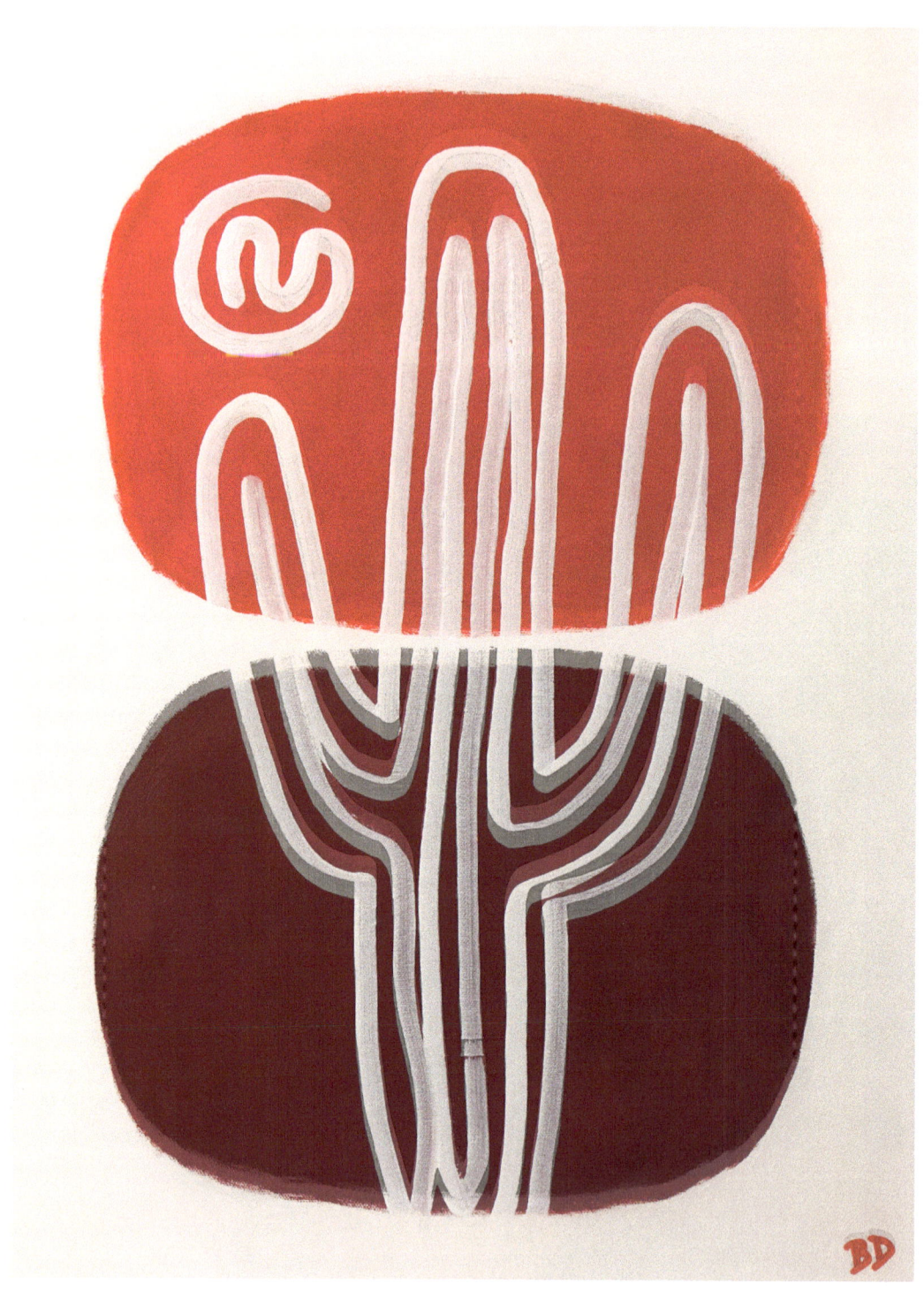

White Saguaro on Red
2018, Acrylic on Canvas, 18 x 24 inches (45.72 x 60.96 cm)

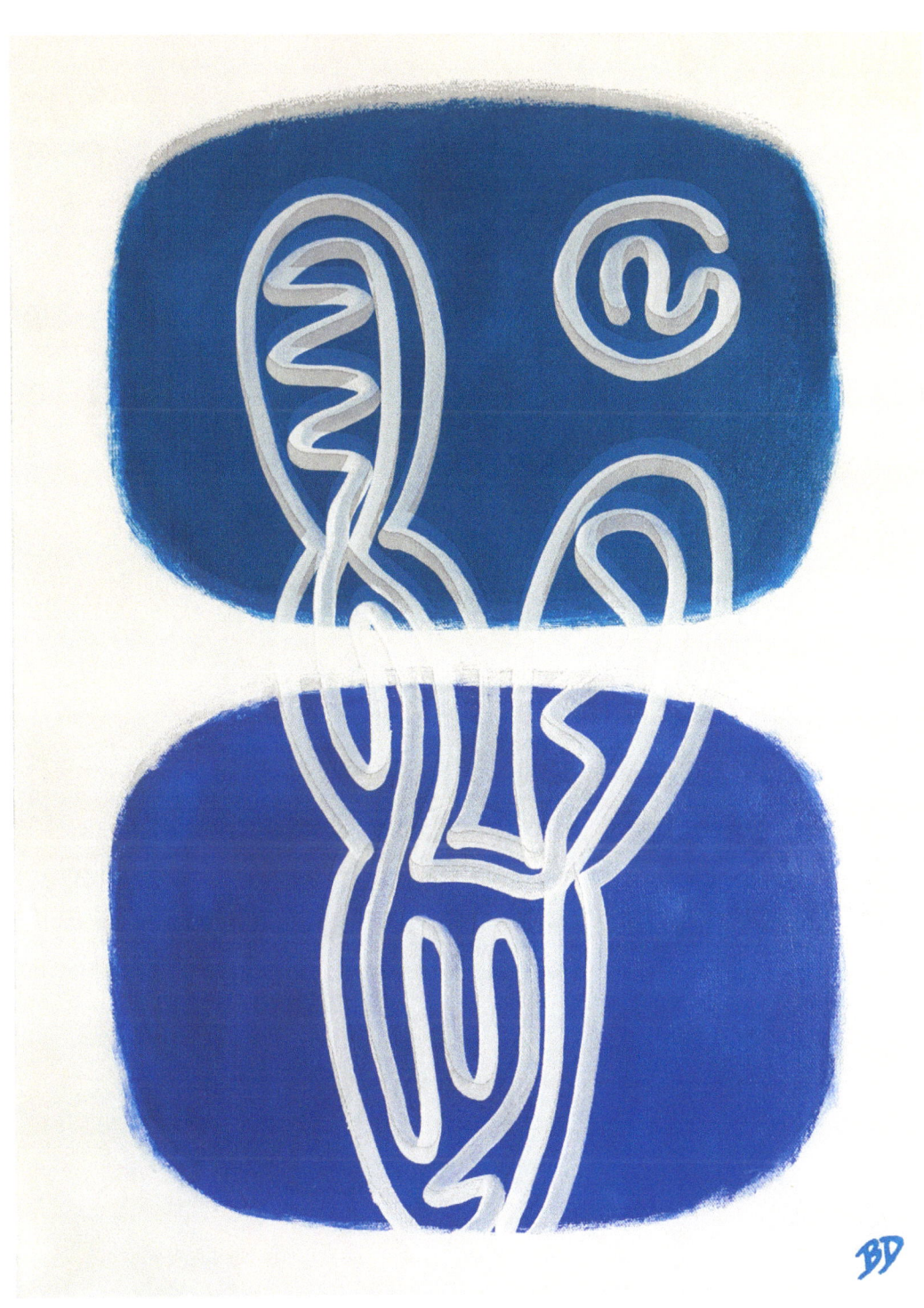

White Prickly Pear on Blue
2018, Acrylic on Canvas, 18 x 24 inches (45.72 x 60.96 cm)

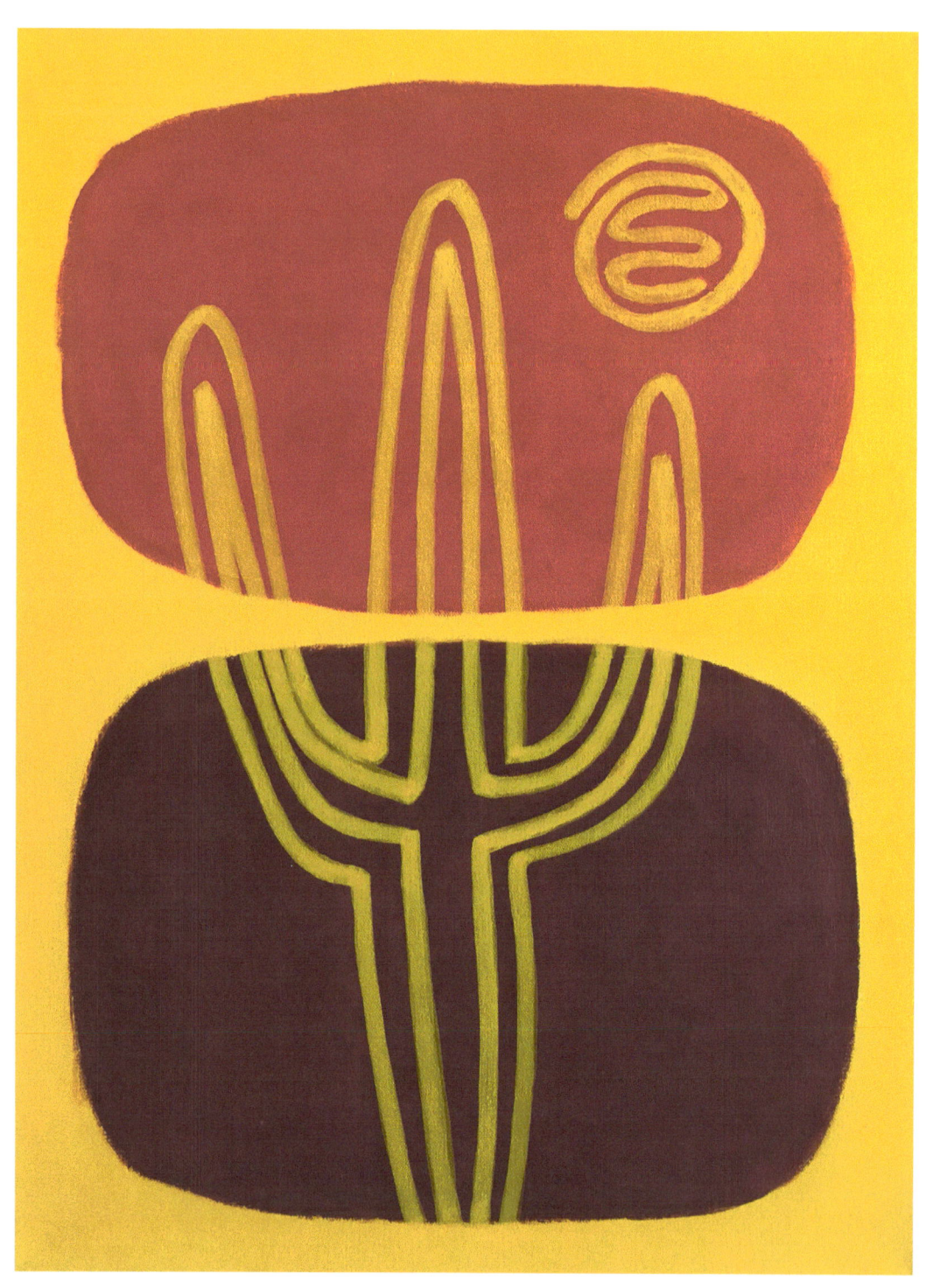

Yellow Saguaro
2018, Acrylic on Canvas, 18 x 24 inches (45.72 x 60.96 cm)

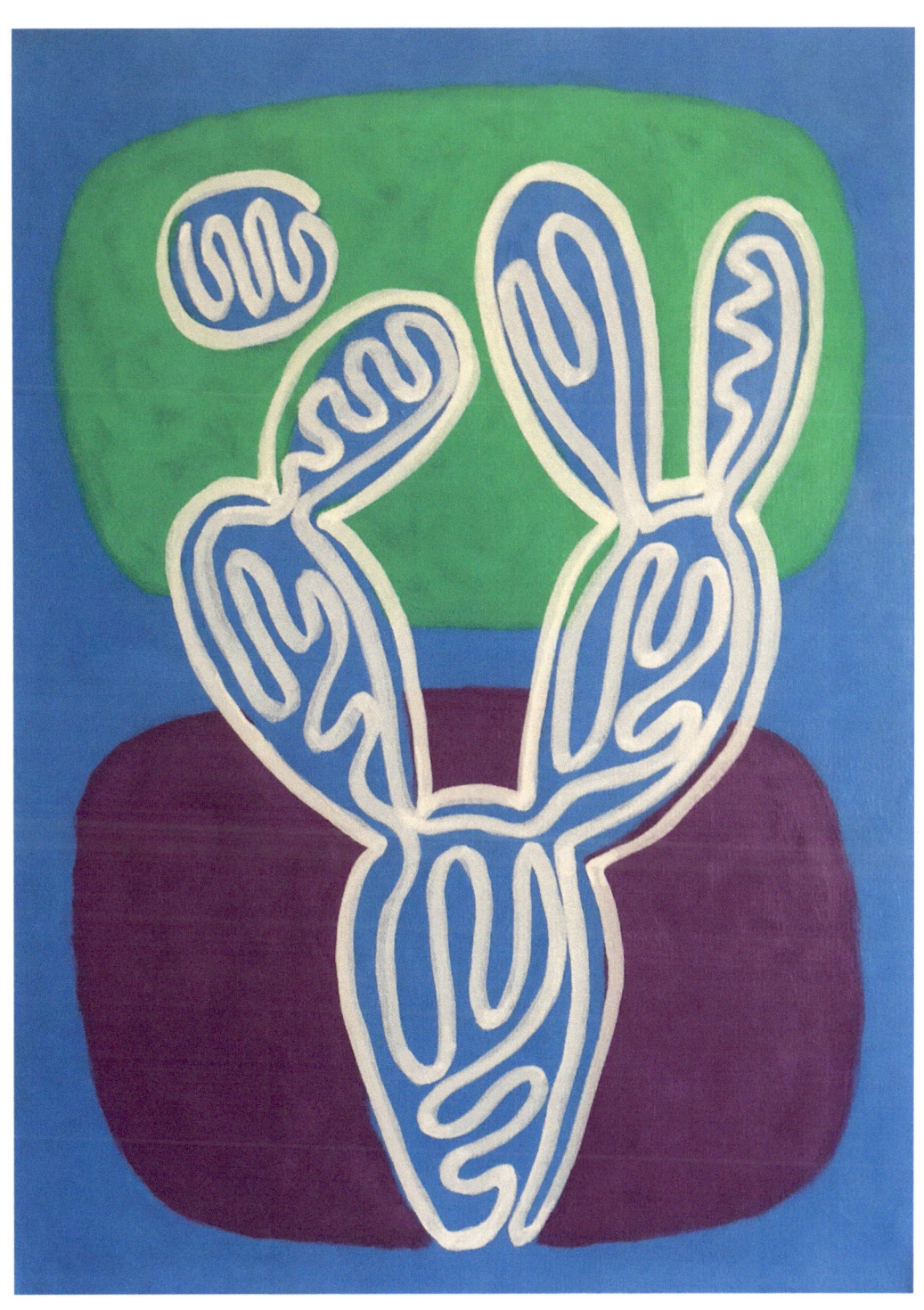

White Prickly Pear on Blue, Green and Purple
2018, Acrylic on Canvas, 18 x 24 inches (45.72 x 60.96 cm)

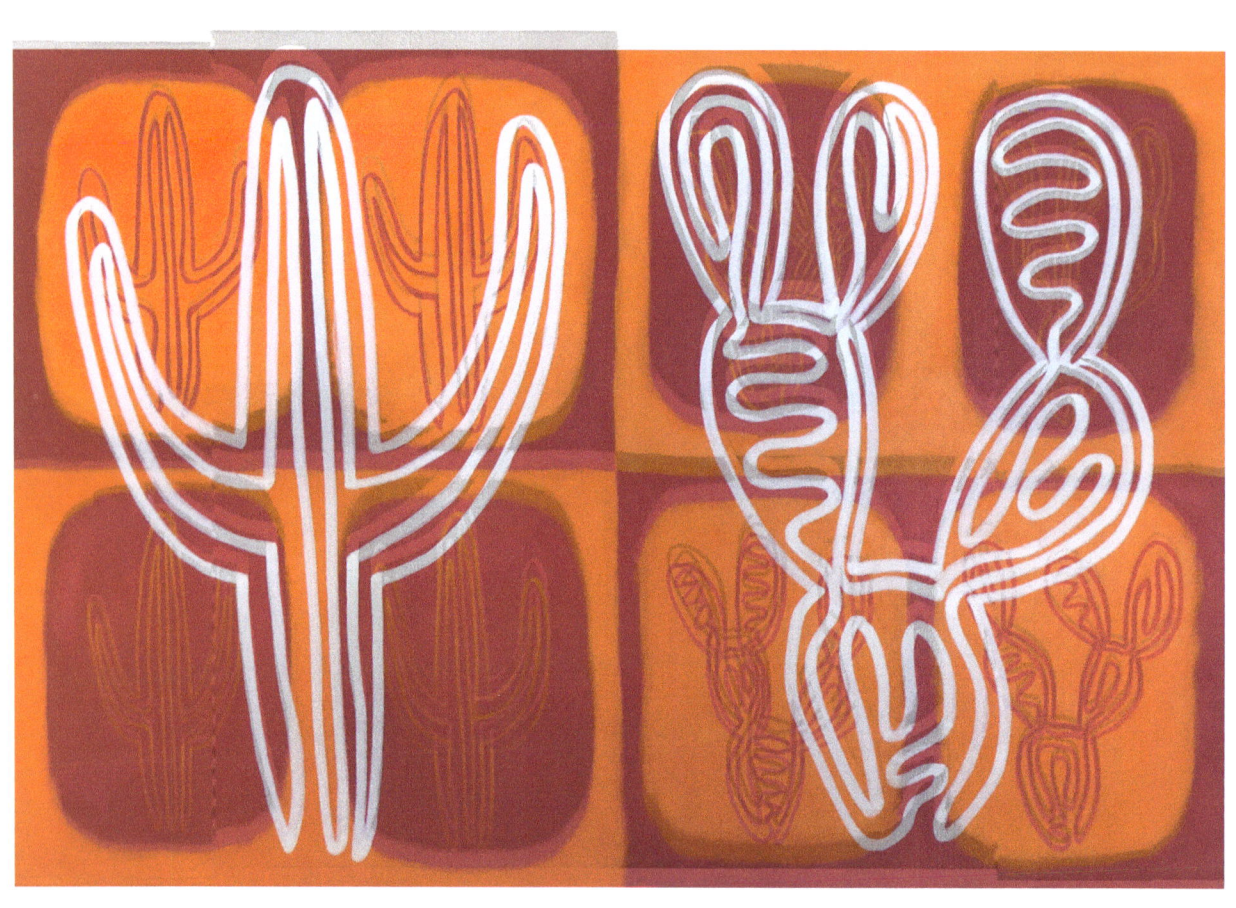

White Saguaro and Prickly Pear on Orange and Red
2018, Acrylic on Canvas, 24 x 36 inches (60.96 x 91.44 cm)

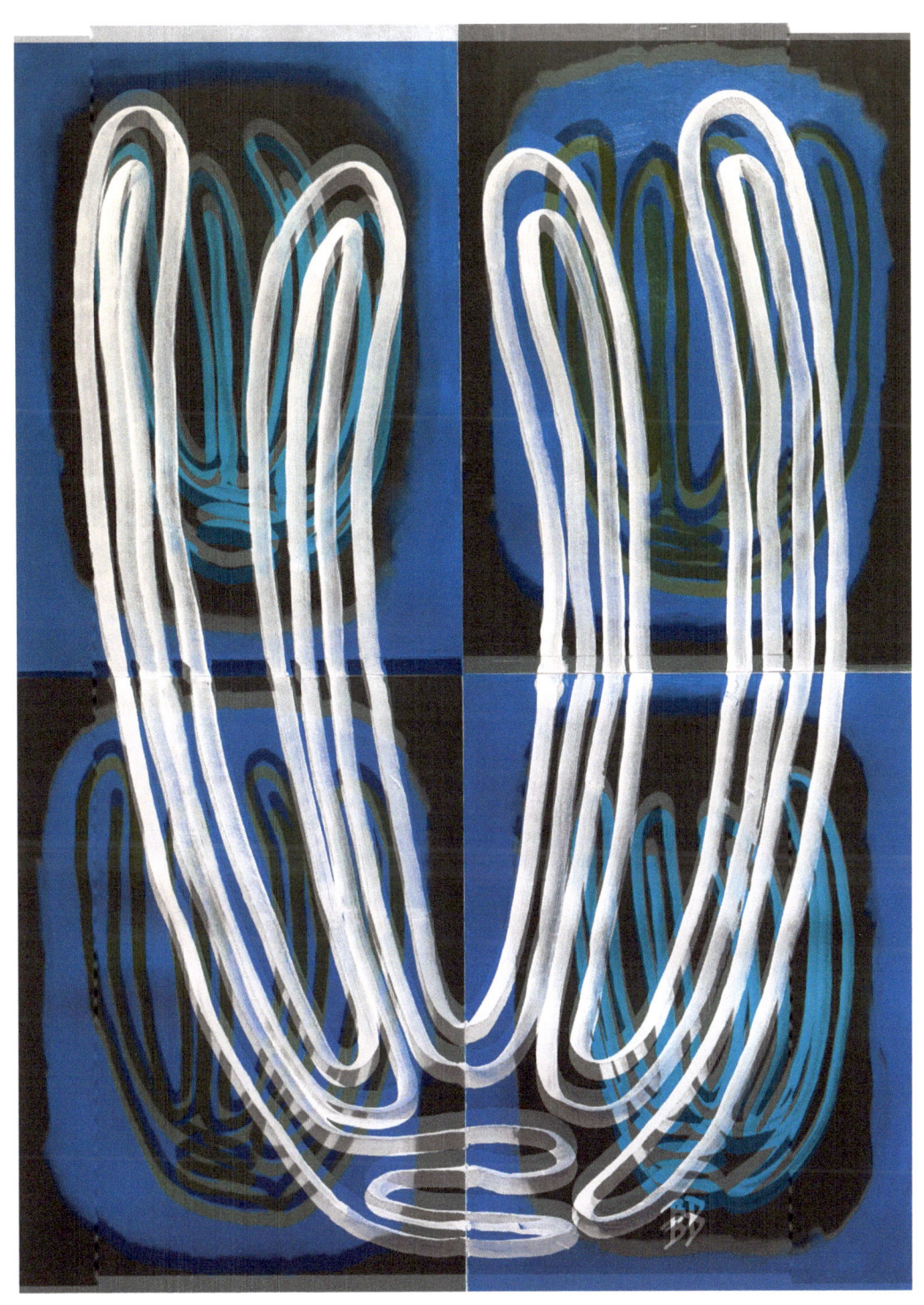

White Organ Pipe on Blue and Green
2018, Acrylic on Paper, 18 x 24 inches (45.72 x 60.96 cm)

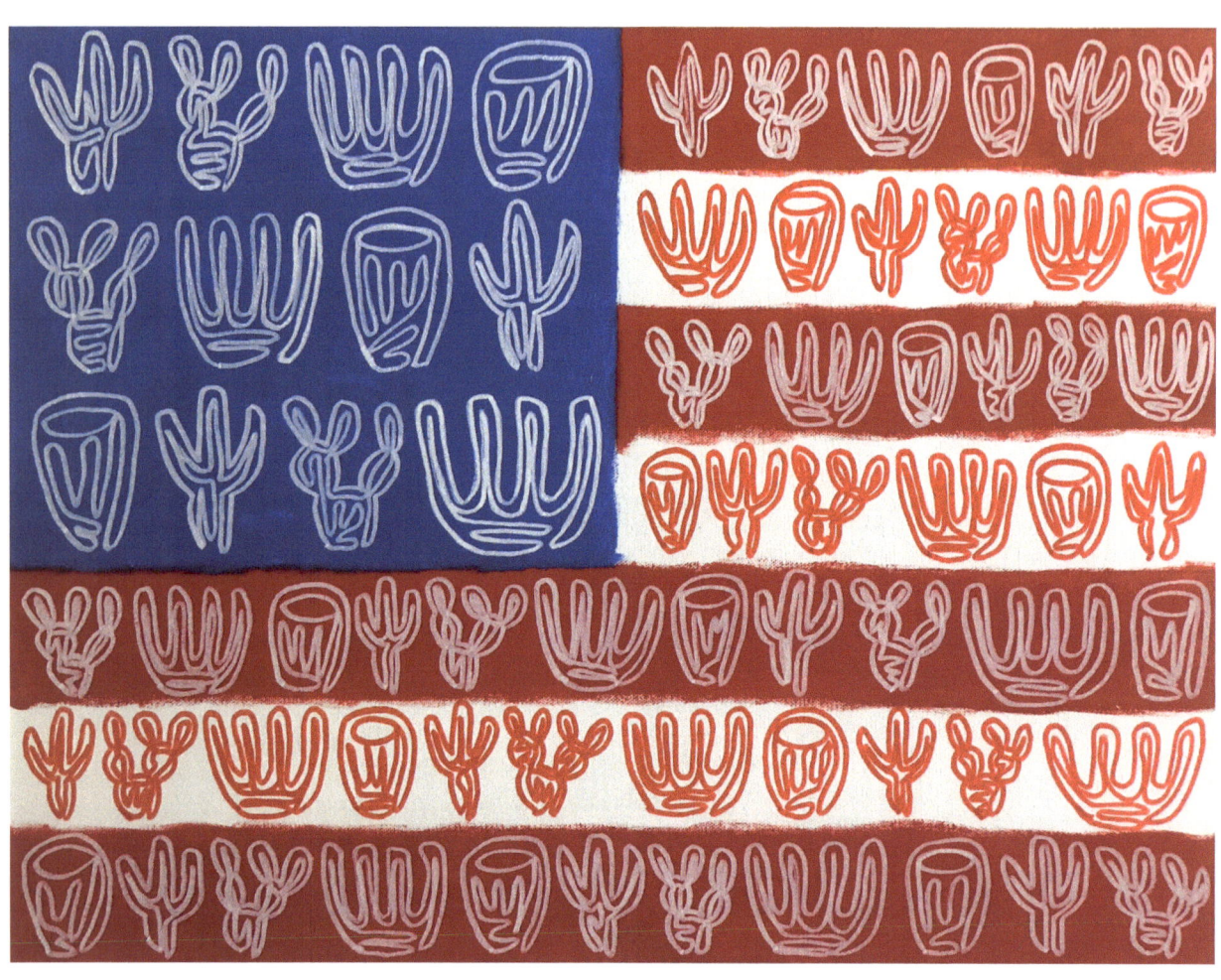

American Cacti
2018, Acrylic on Canvas, 18 x 24 inches (45.72 x 60.96 cm)

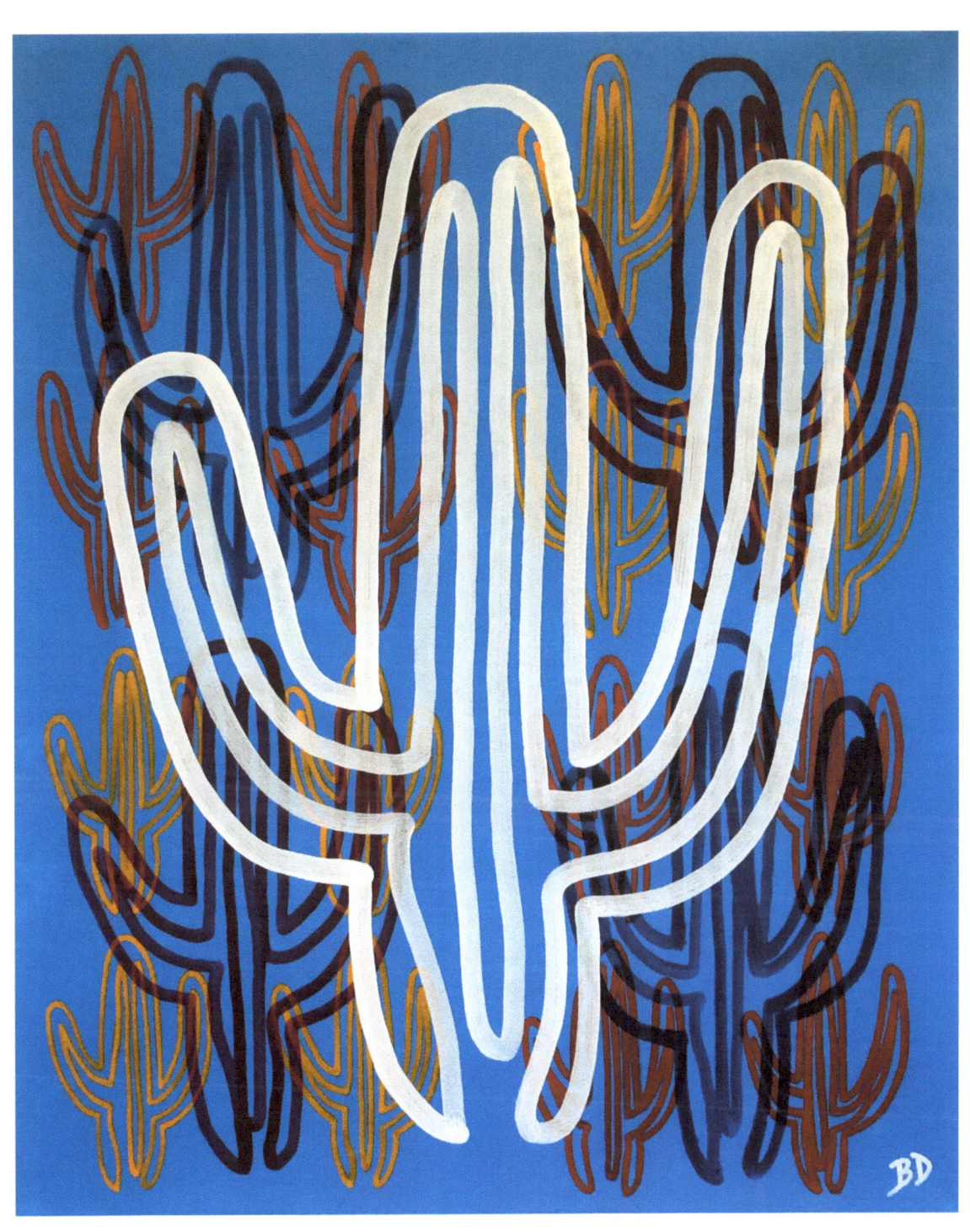

21 Saguaros
2019, Acrylic on Canvas, 20 x 24 inches (50.8 x 60.96 cm)

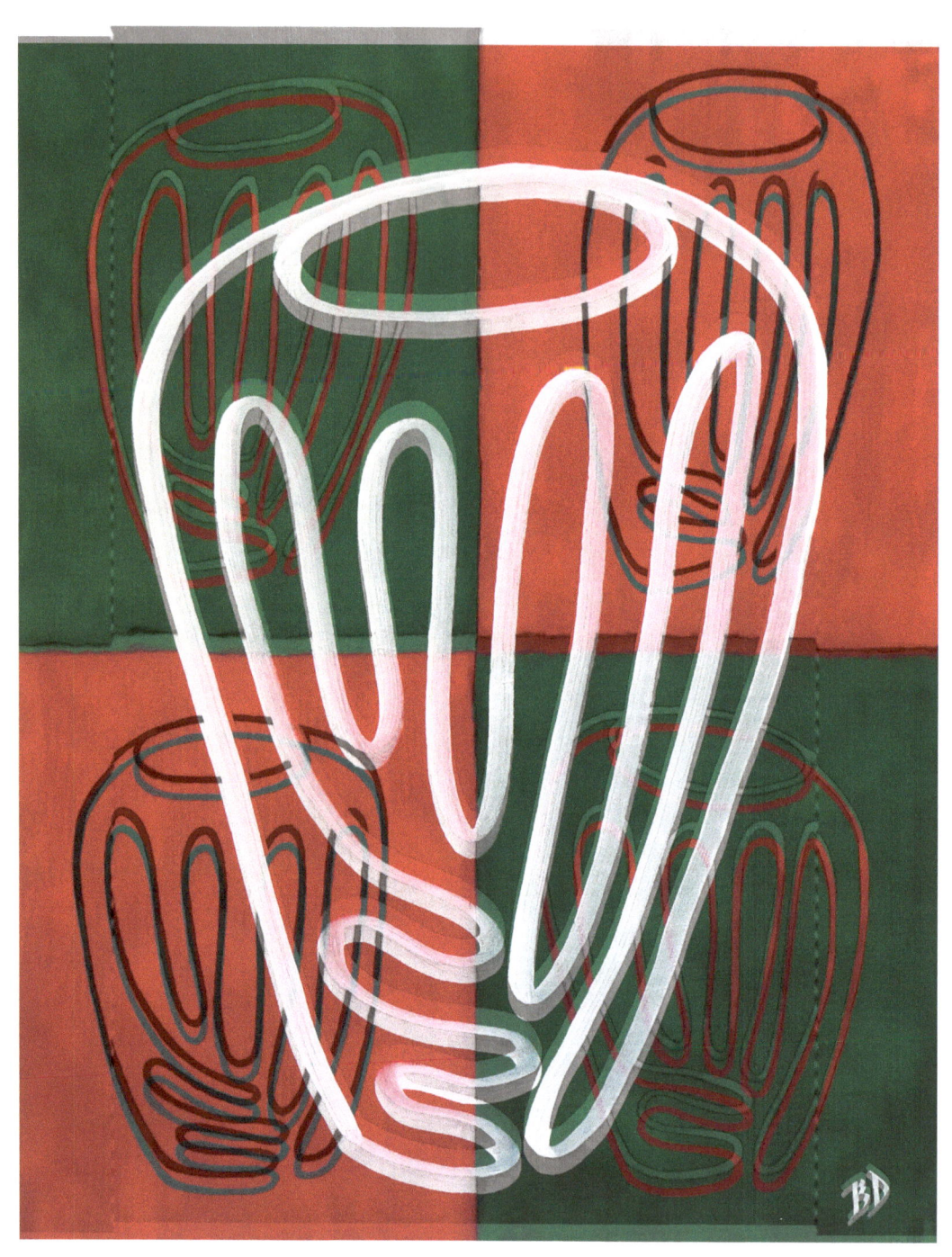

White Barrel Cacti
2018, Acrylic on Wood Panel, 16 x 20 inches (40.64 x 50.8 cm)

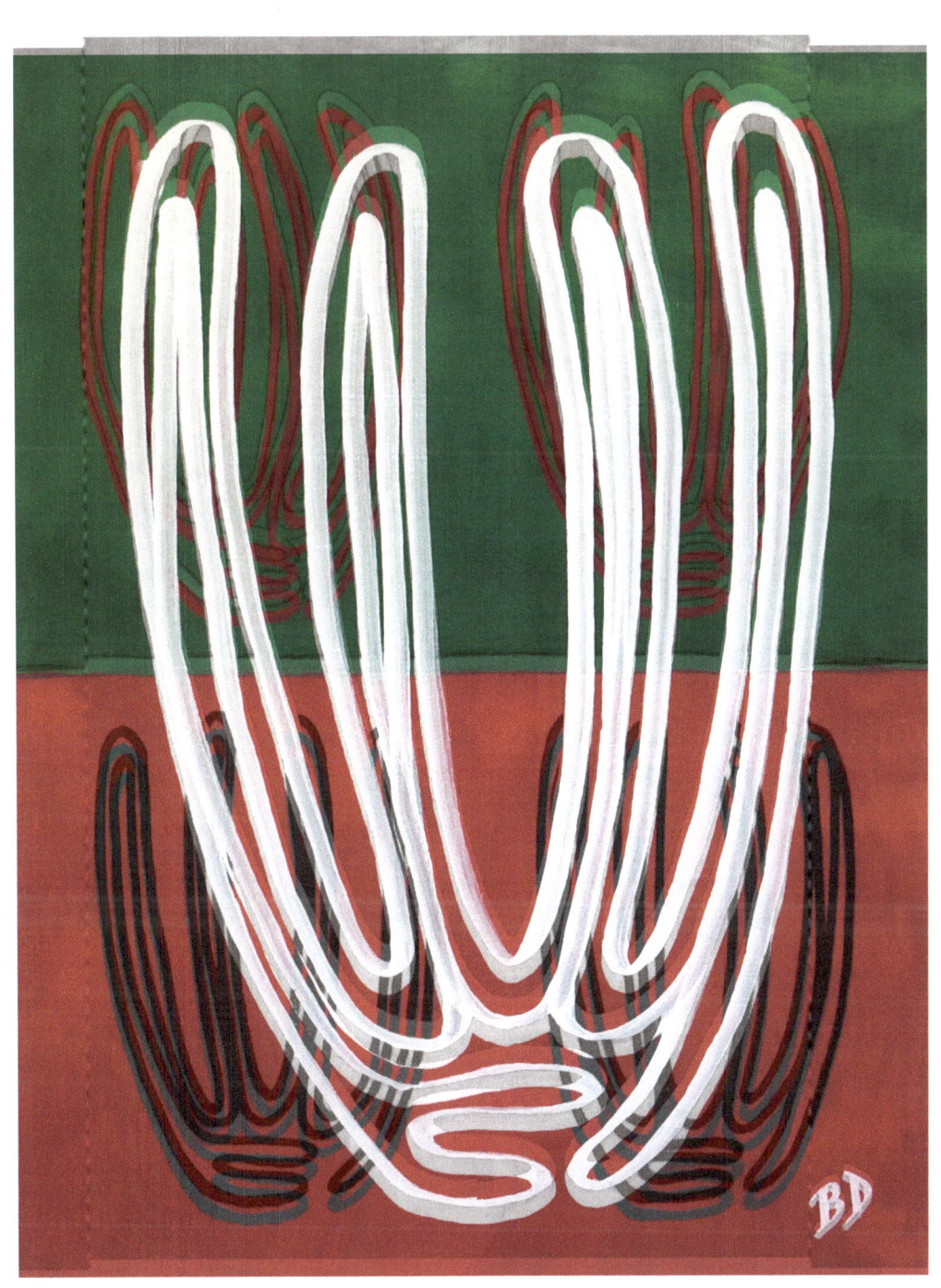

White Organ Pipe
2018, Acrylic on Wood Panel, 11 x 14 inches (27.94 x 35.56 cm)

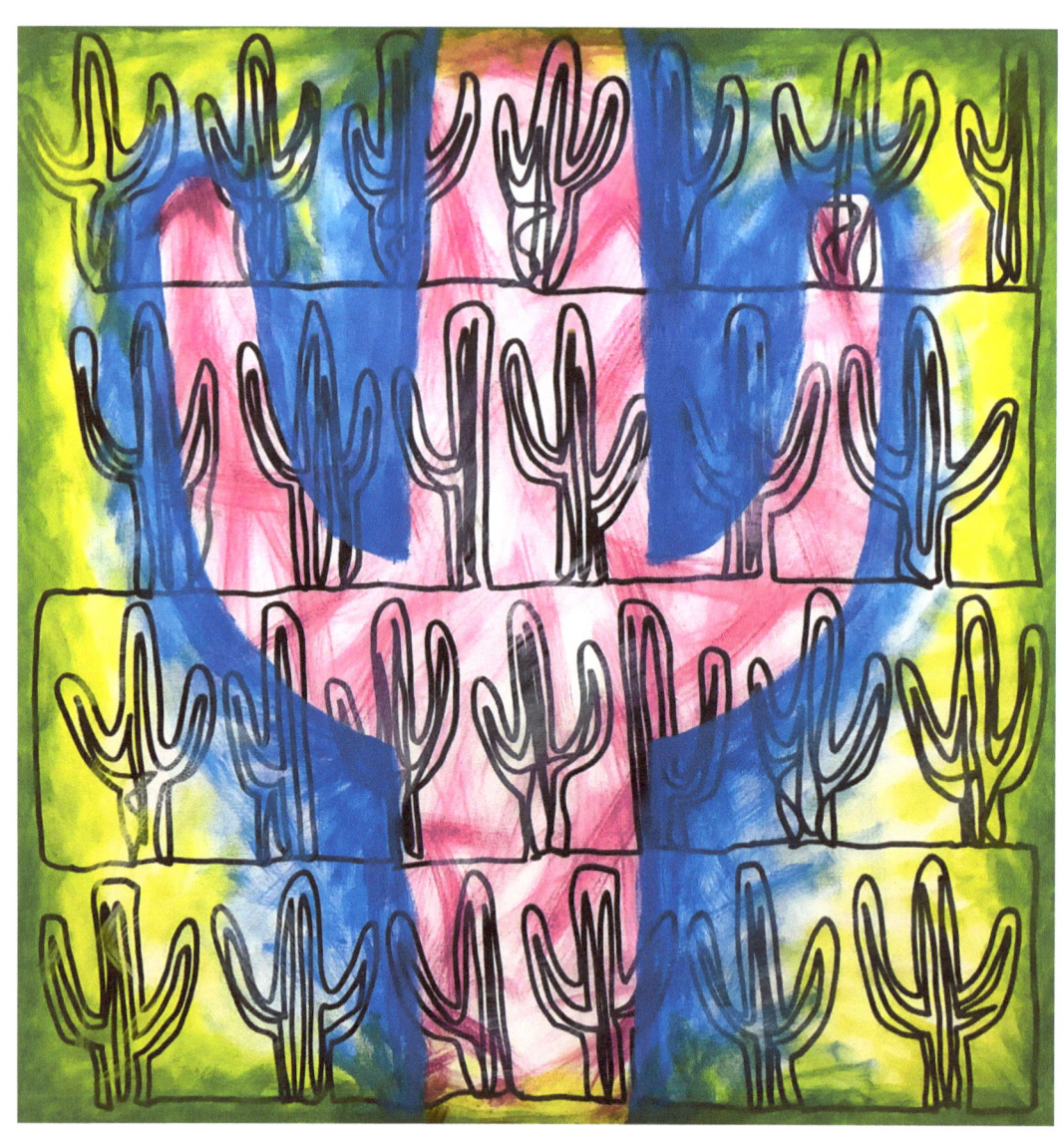

Saguaro Spirit
2018, Acrylic on Canvas, 24 x 24 inches (60.96 x 60.96 cm)

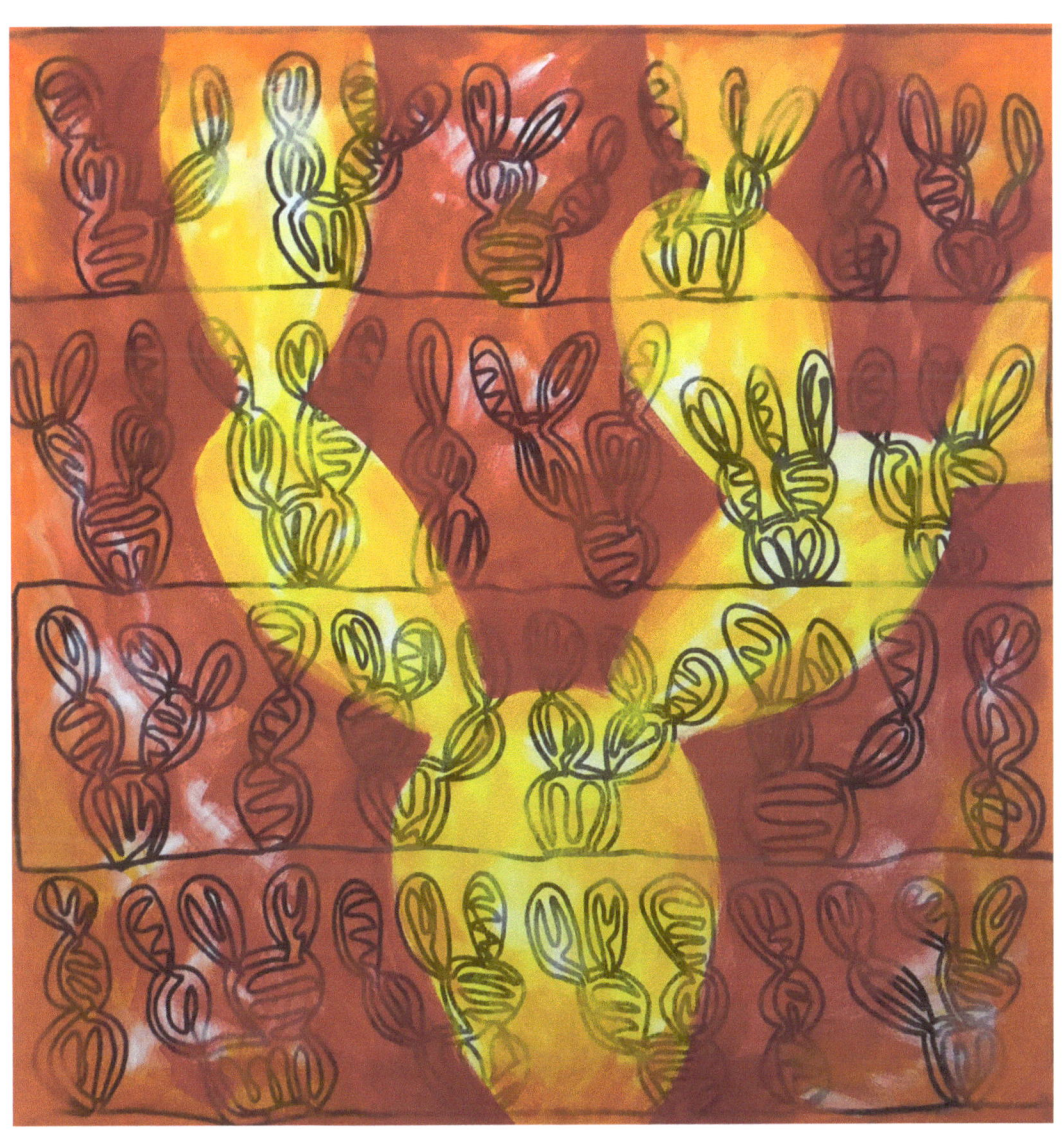

Prickly Pear Heat
2018, Acrylic on Canvas, 24 x 24 inches (60.96 x 60.96 cm)

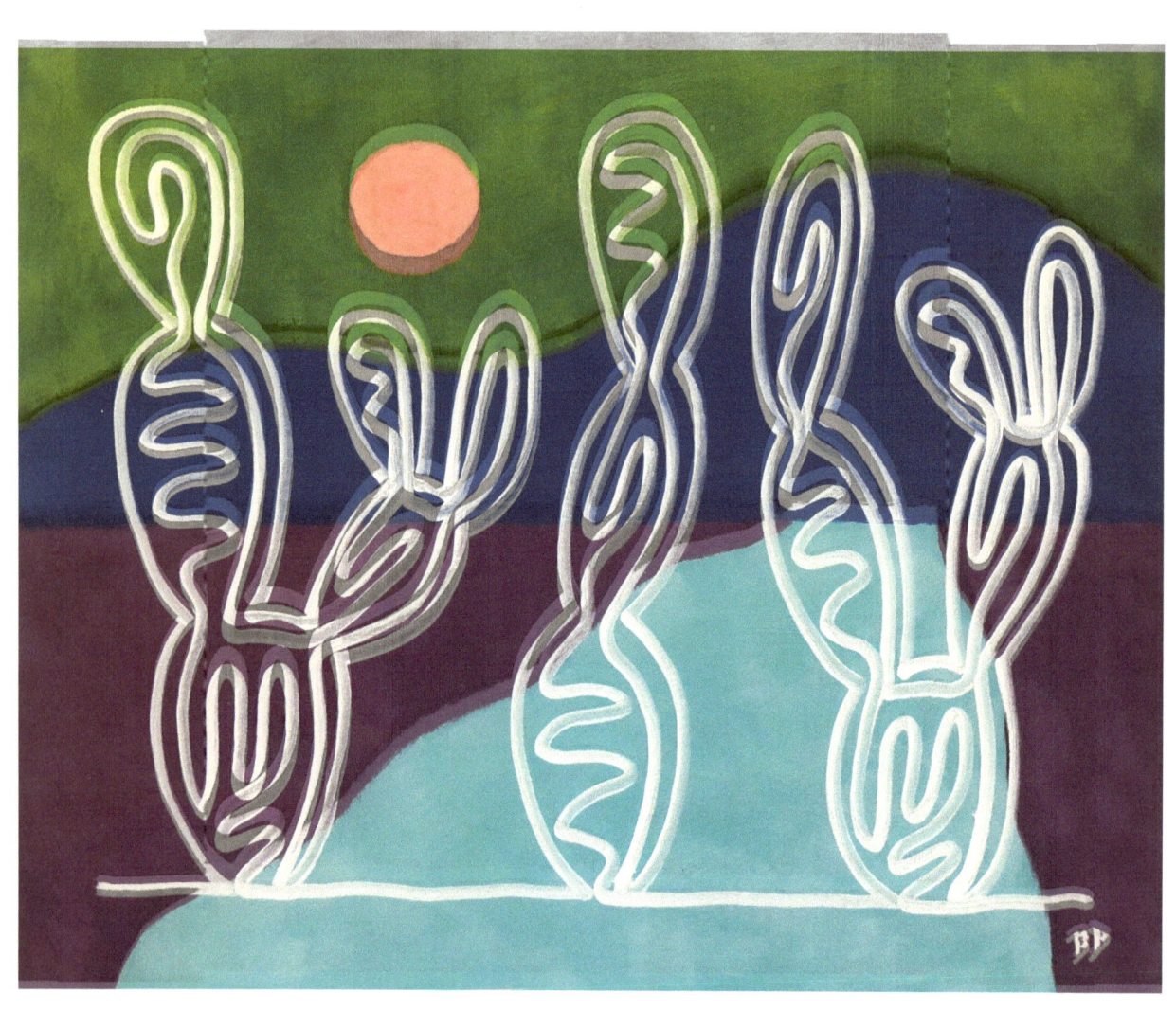

Prickly Pear by the River
2018, Acrylic on Wood Panel, 16 x 20 inches (40.64 x 50.8 cm)

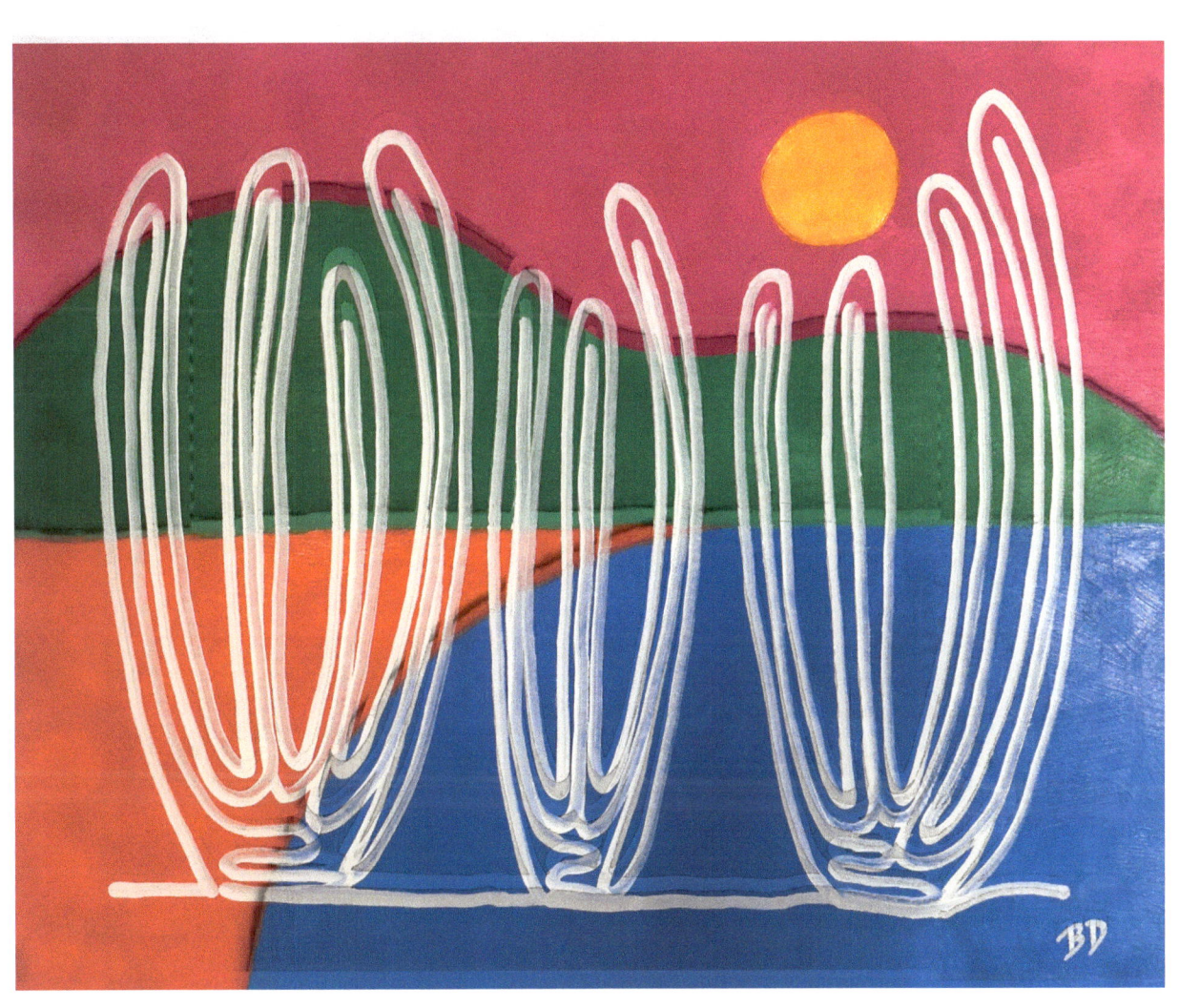

Lakeside Organ Pipe
2018, Acrylic on Wood Panel, 16 x 20 inches (40.64 x 50.8 cm)

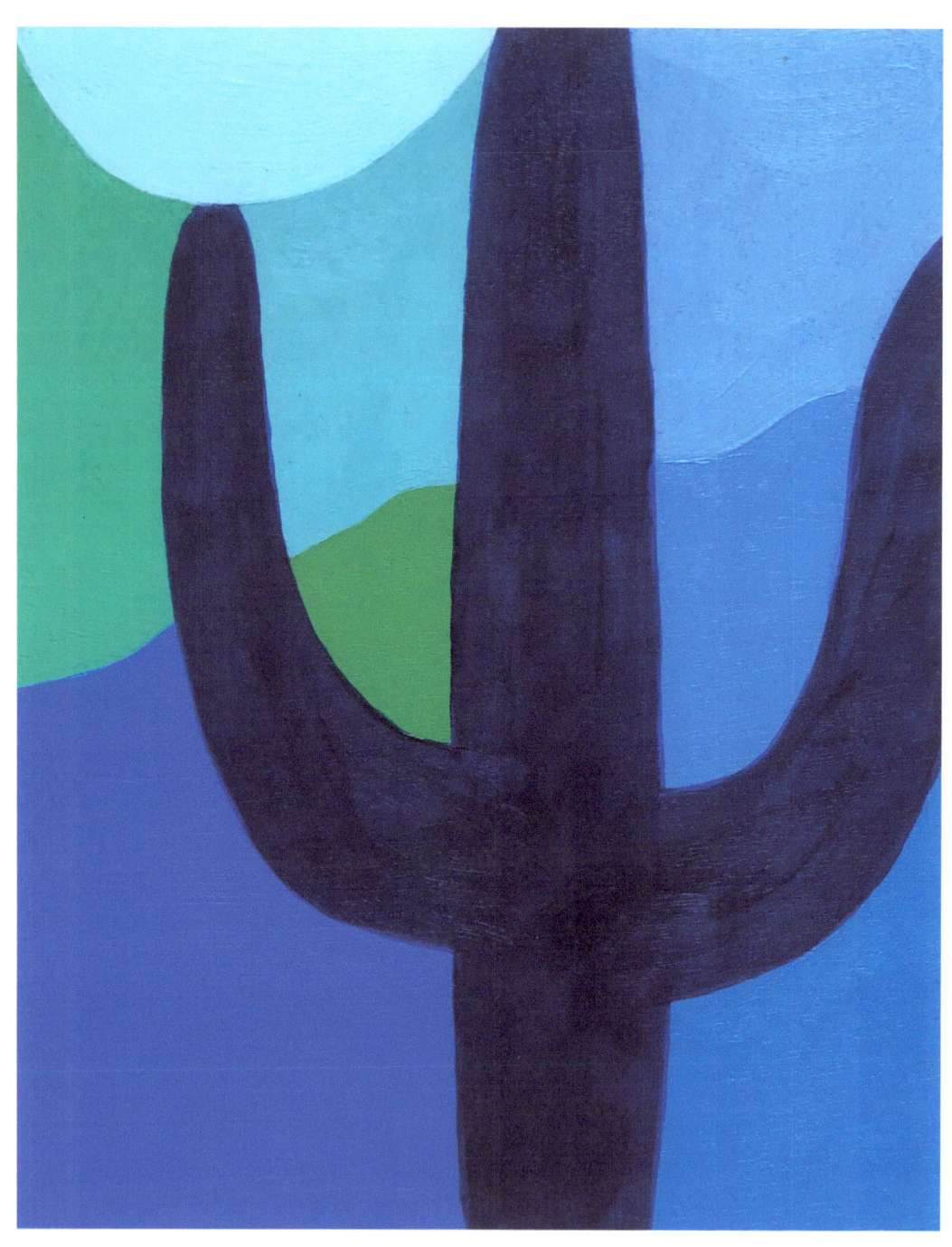

Saguaro Mosaic
2019, Acrylic on Wood Panel, 8 x 10 inches (20.32 x 25.4 cm)

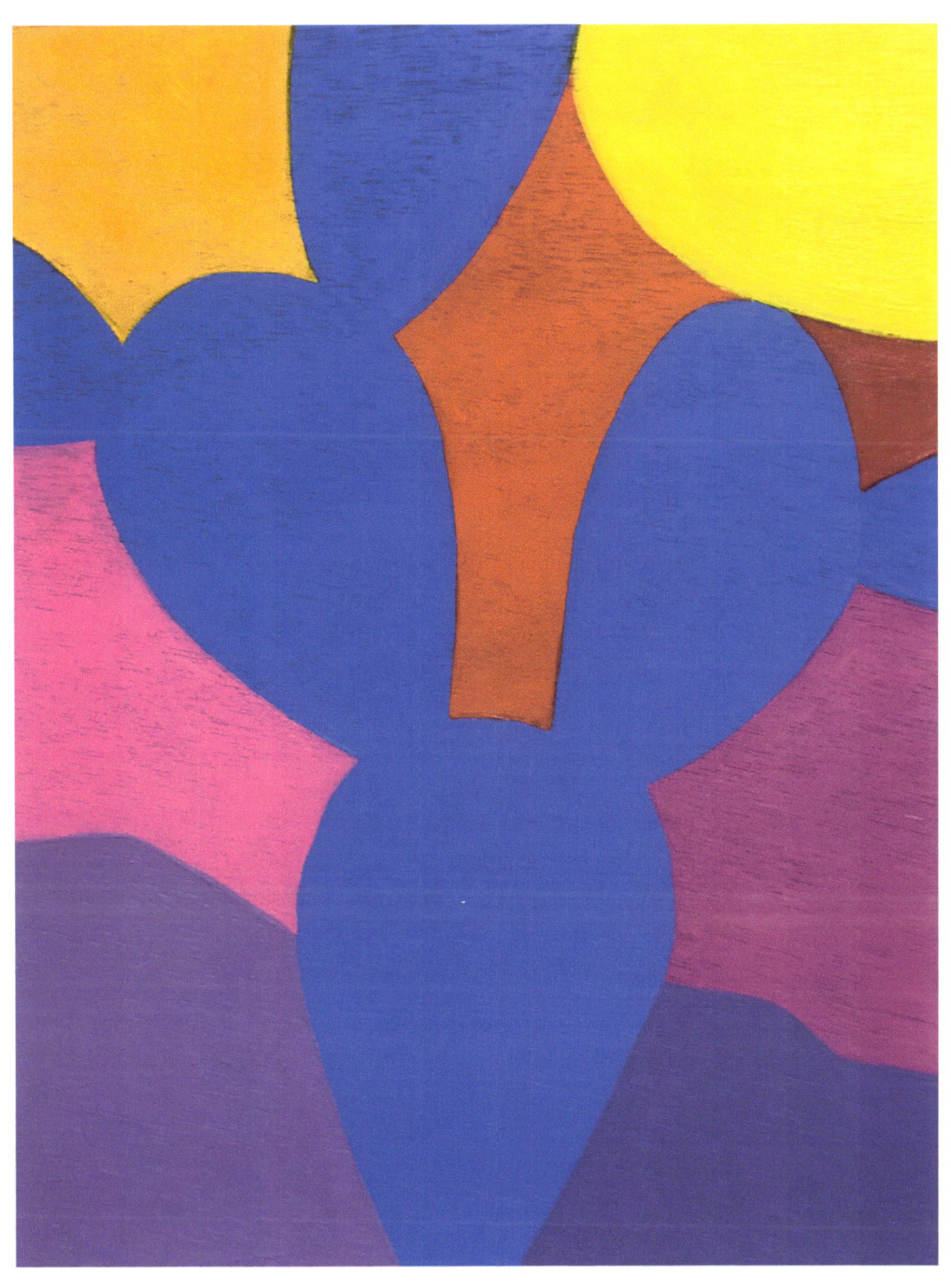

Prickly Pear Mosaic
2019, Acrylic on Wood Panel, 8 x 10 inches (20.32 x 25.4 cm)

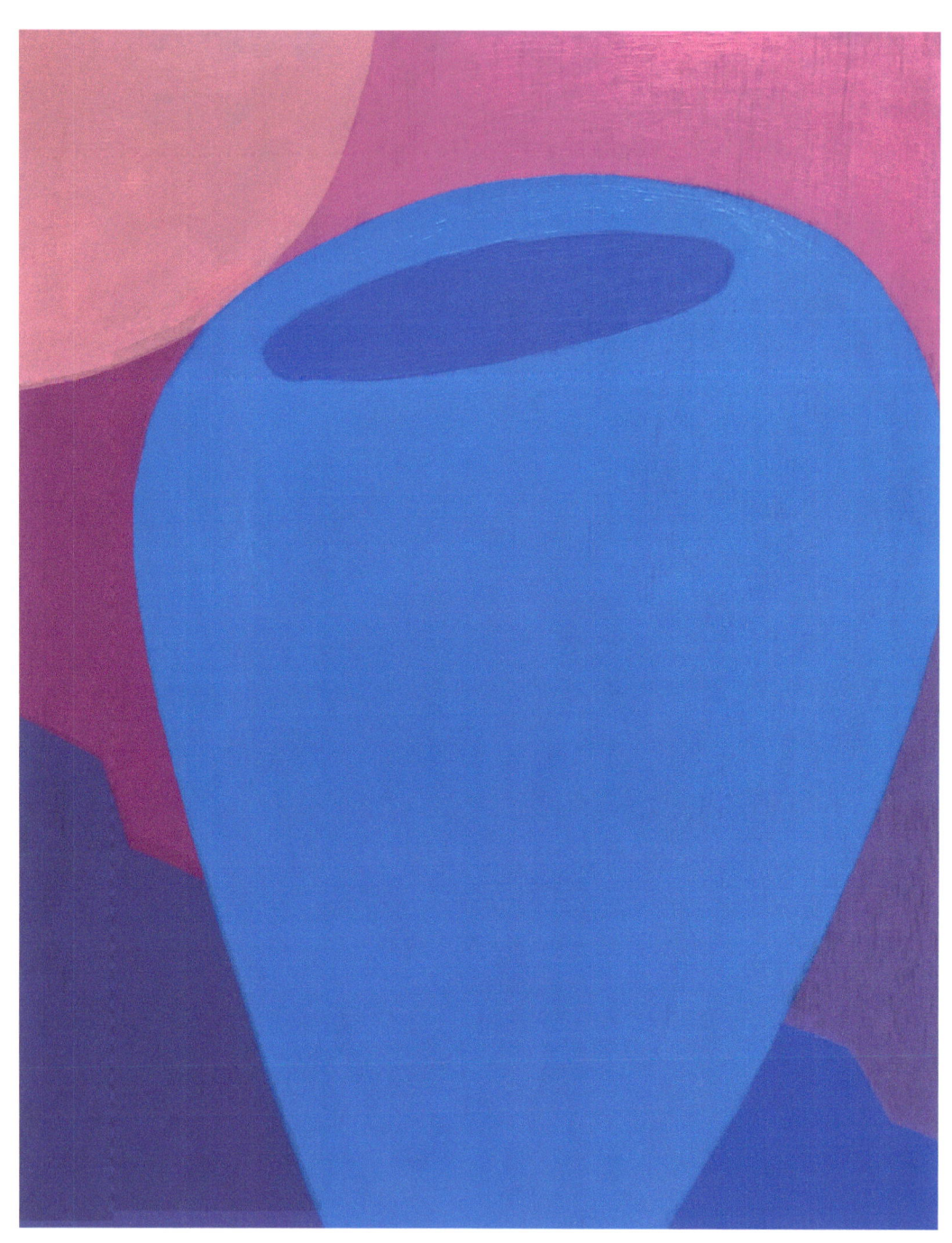

Barrel Cactus Mosaic
2019, Acrylic on Wood Panel, 8 x 10 inches (20.32 x 25.4 cm)

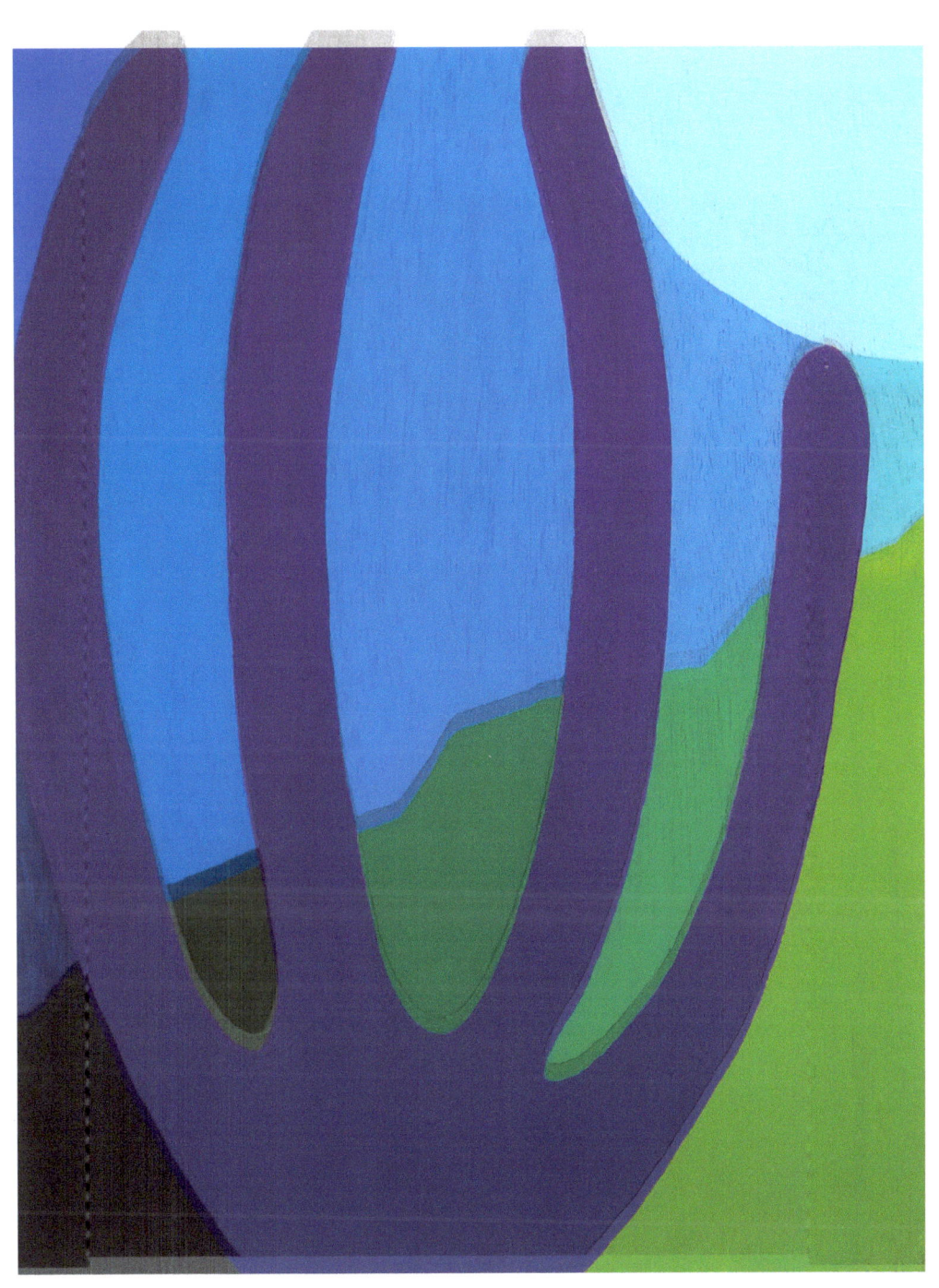

Organ Pipe Mosaic
2019, Acrylic on Wood Panel, 8 x 10 inches (20.32 x 25.4 cm)

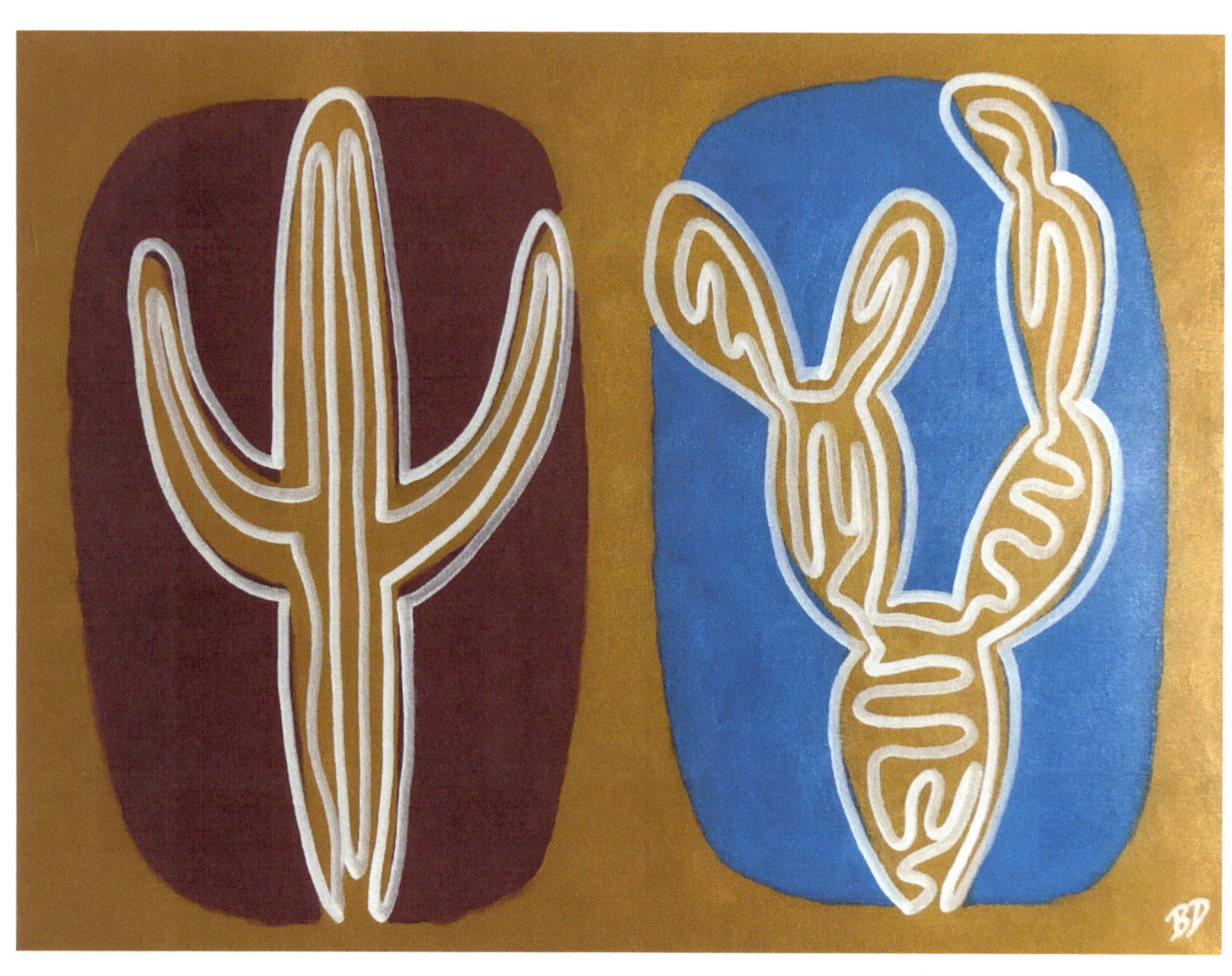

Saguaro and Prickly Pear
2018, Acrylic on Canvas, 18 x 24 inches (45.72 x 60.96 cm)

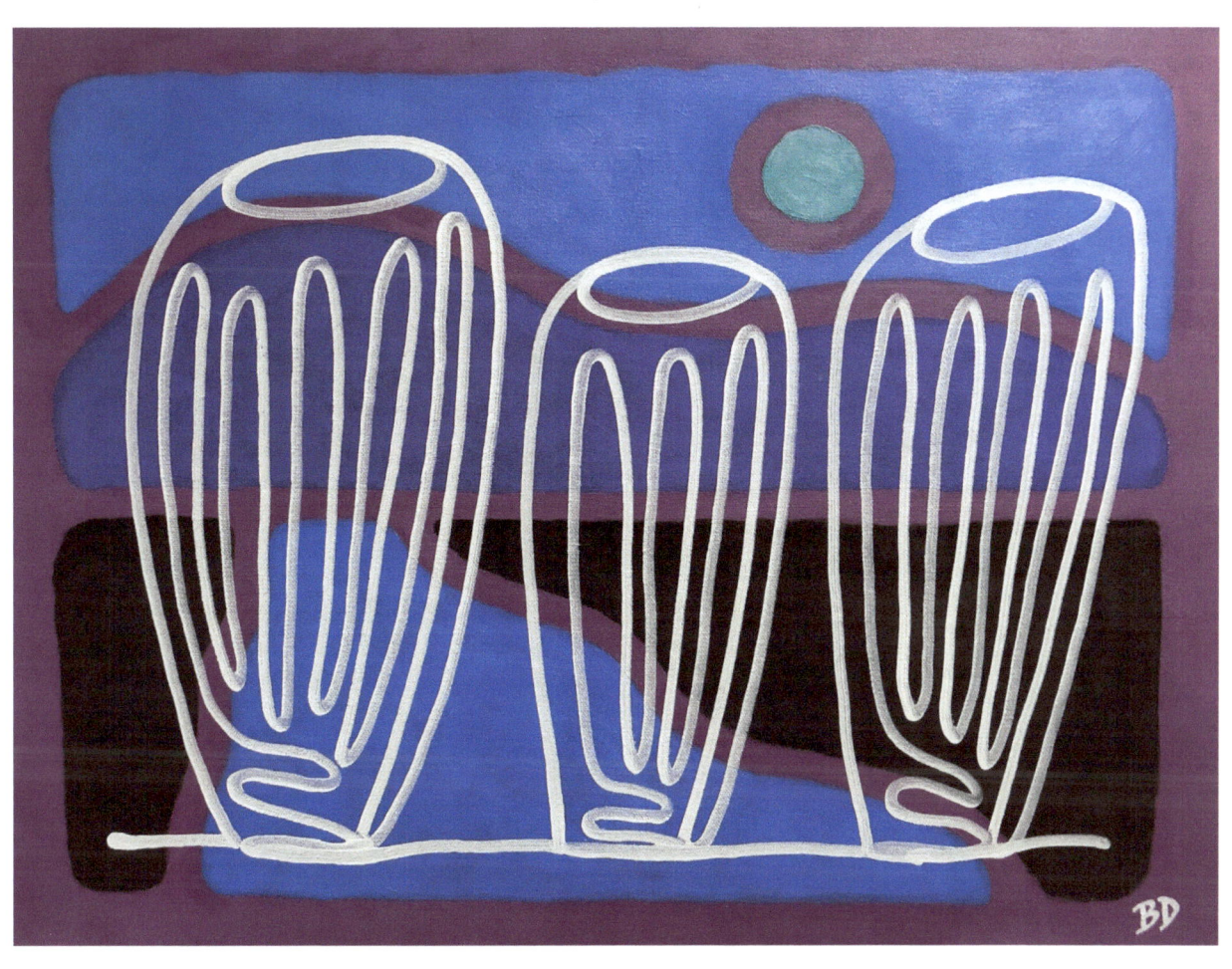

Barrels on the Canal
2018, Acrylic on Canvas, 18 x 24 inches (45.72 x 60.96 cm)

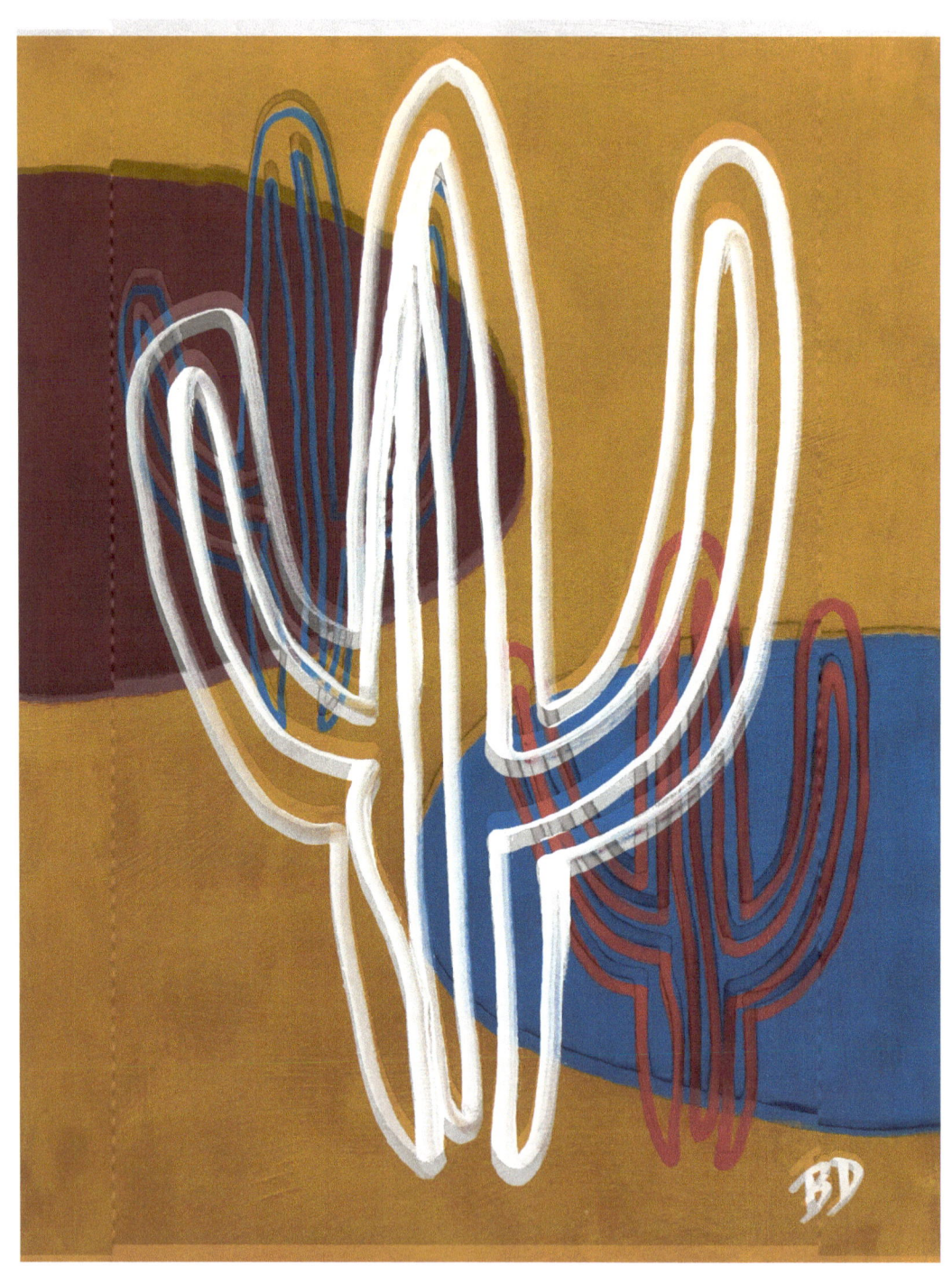

White Saguaro on Red, Blue and Yellow
2018, Acrylic on Wood Panel, 11 x 14 inches (27.94 x 35.56 cm)

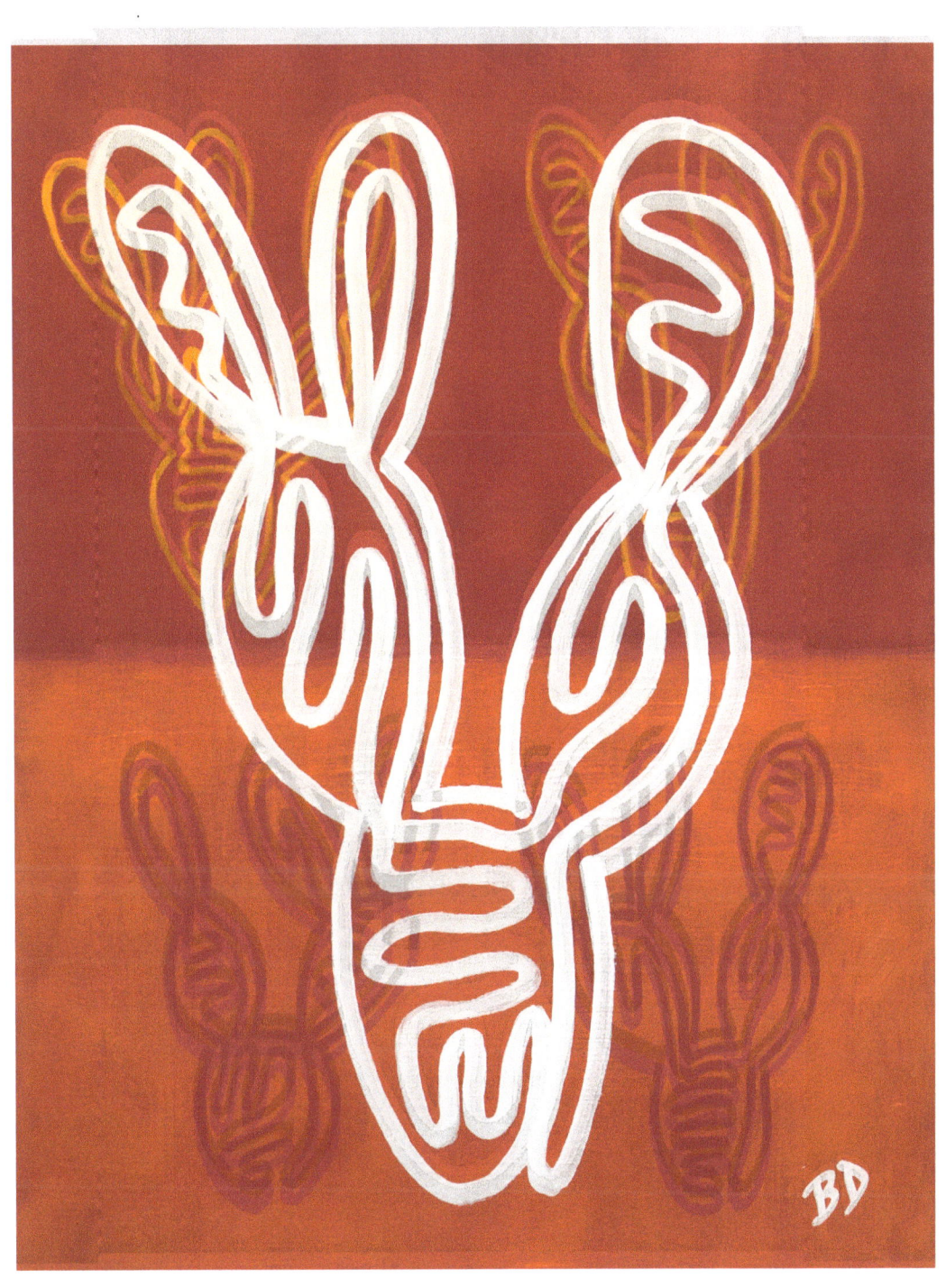

White Prickly Pear on Red and Orange
2018, Acrylic on Wood Panel, 11 x 14 inches (27.94 x 35.56 cm)

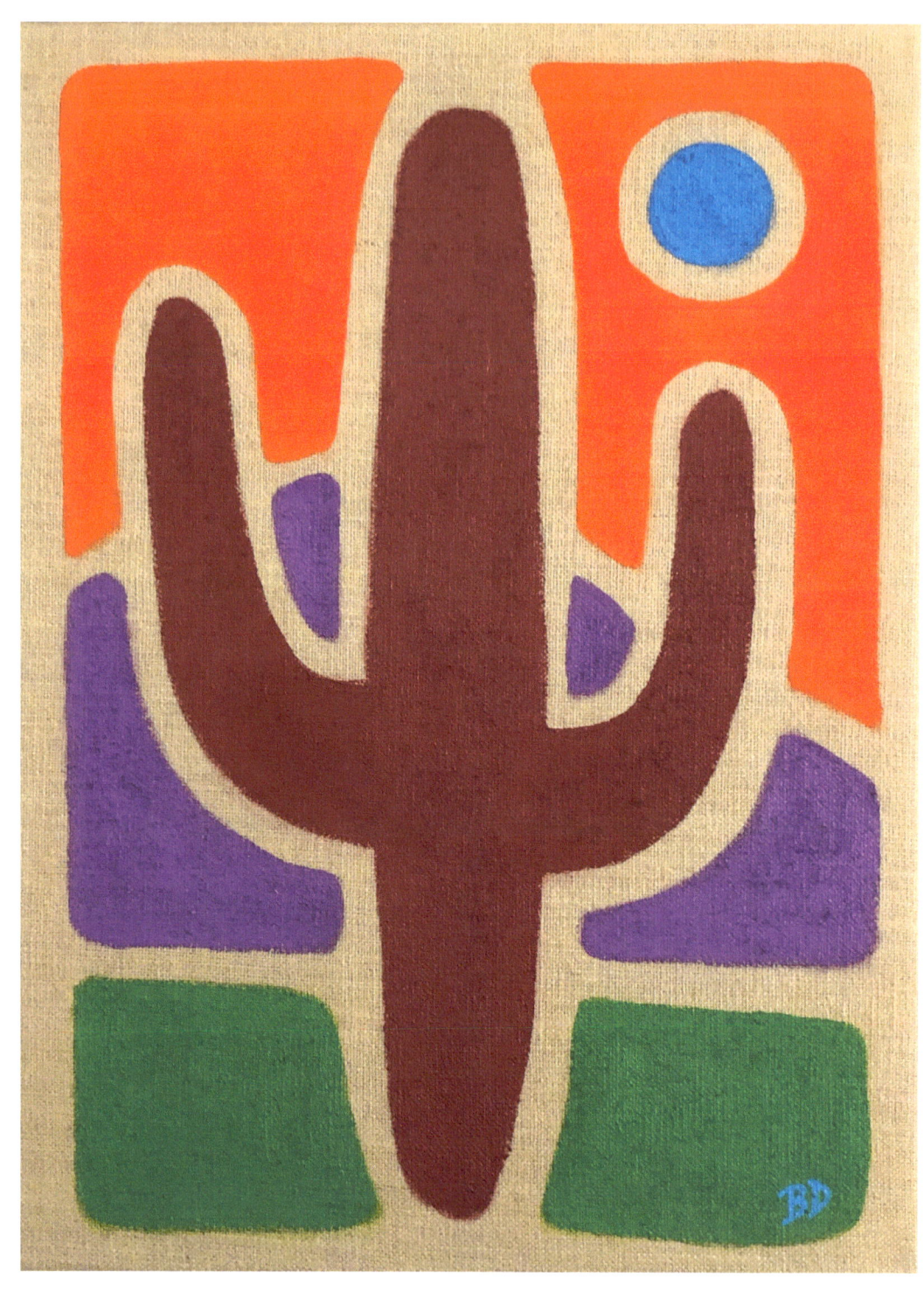

Maroon Saguaro
2020, Acrylic on Burlap Canvas, 18 x 24 inches (45.72 x 60.96 cm)

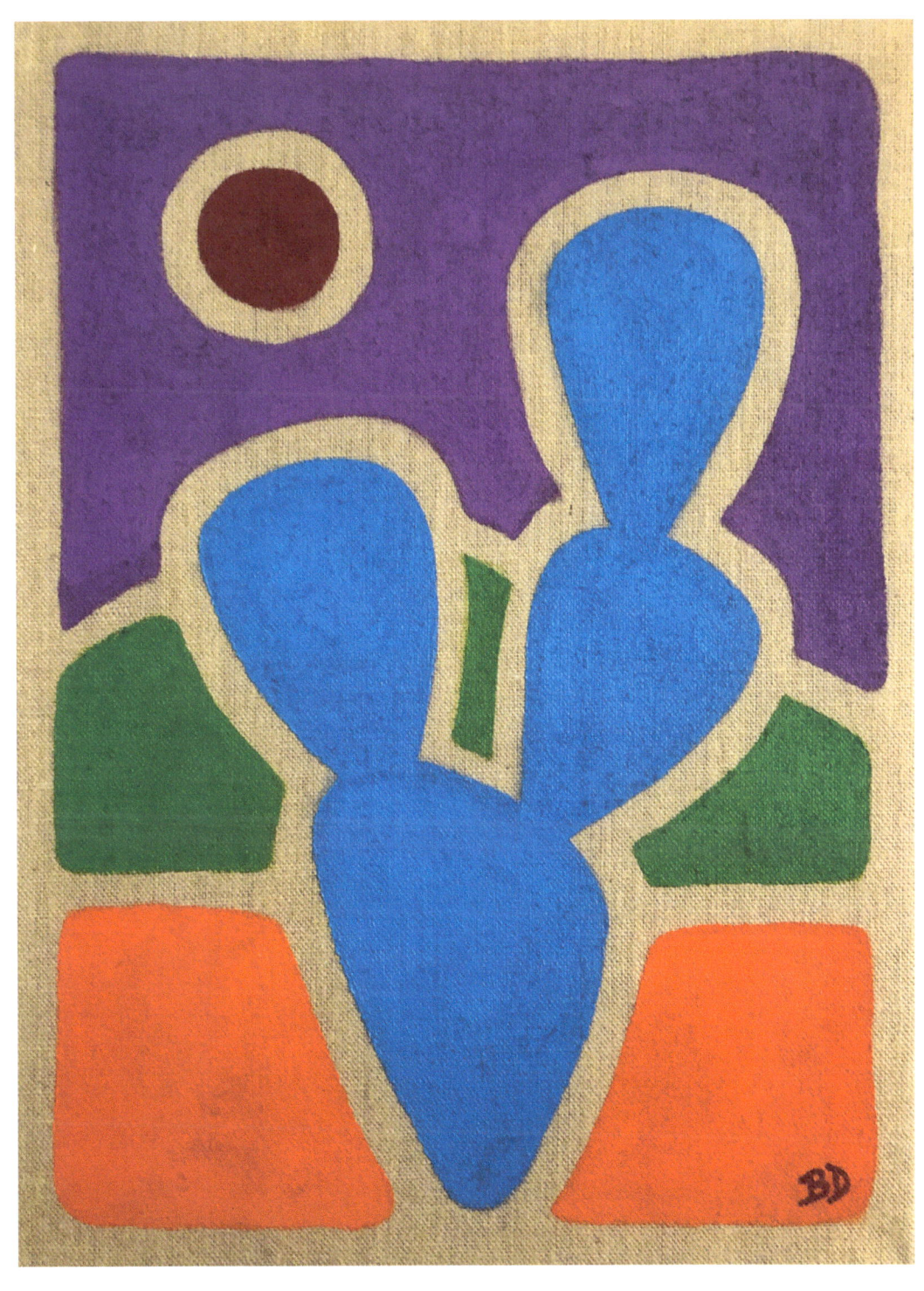

Blue Prickly Pear
2020, Acrylic on Burlap Canvas, 18 x 24 inches (45.72 x 60.96 cm)

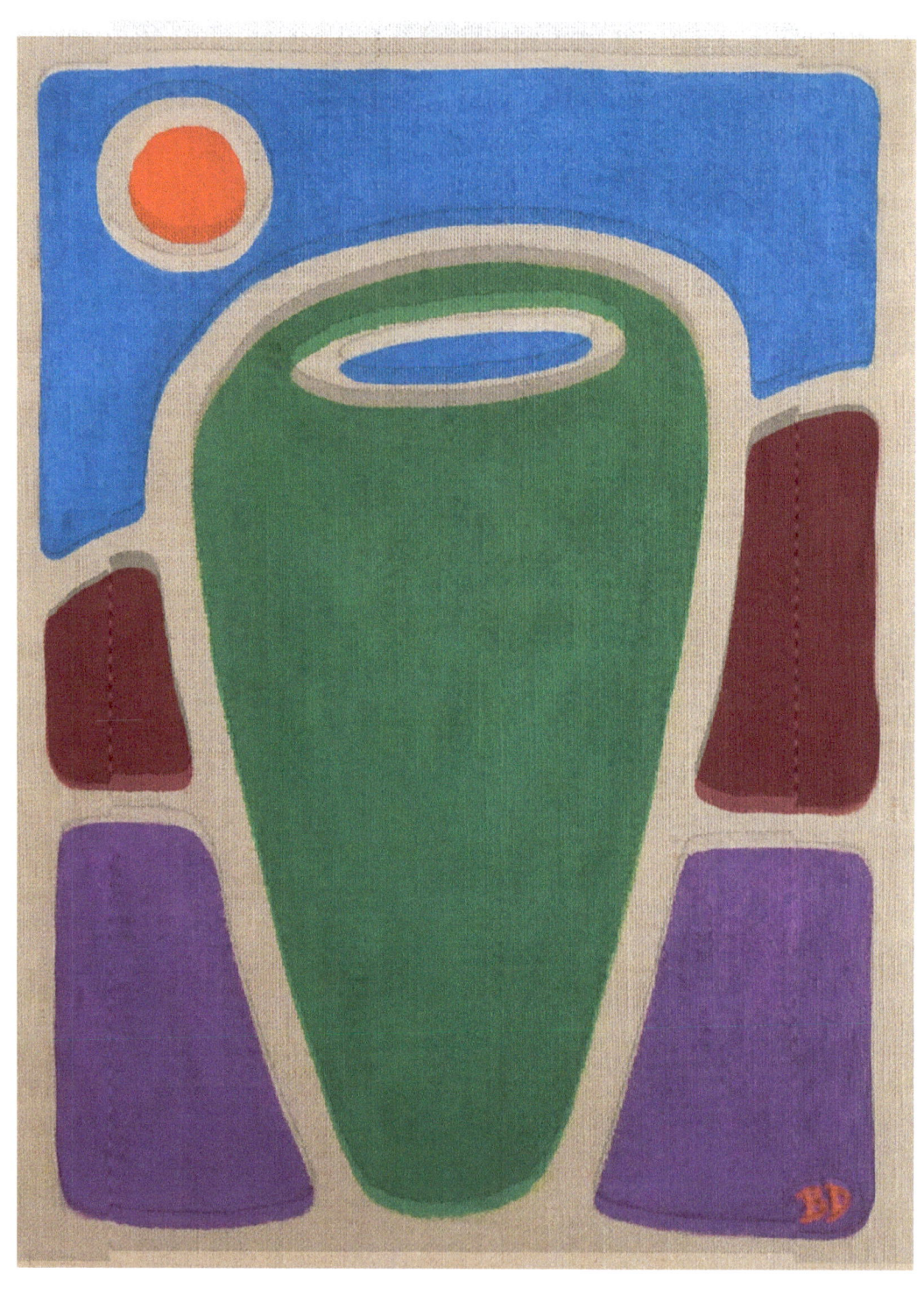

Green Barrel Cactus
2020, Acrylic on Burlap Canvas, 18 x 24 inches (45.72 x 60.96 cm)

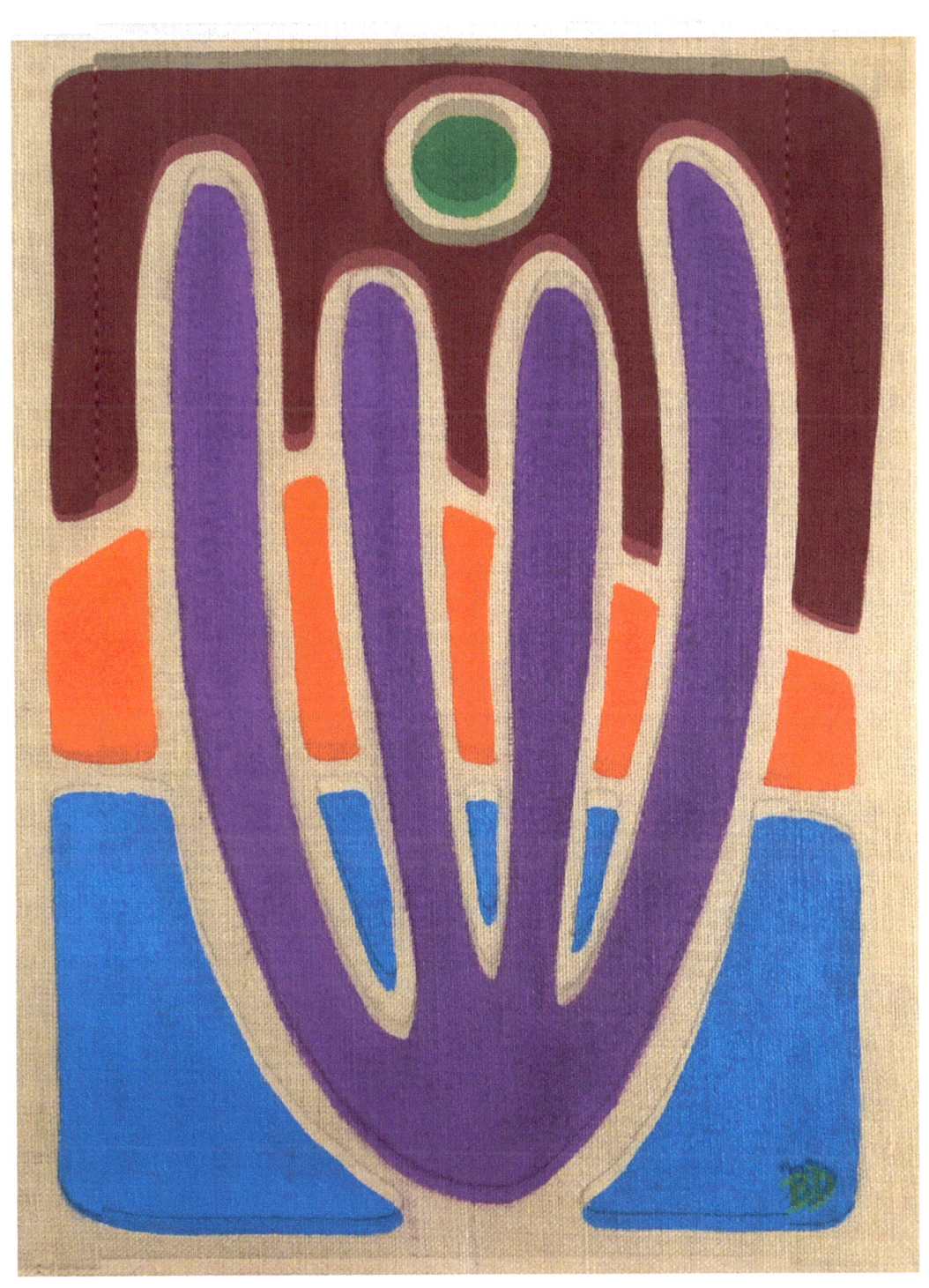

Purple Organ Pipe
2020, Acrylic on Burlap Canvas, 18 x 24 inches (45.72 x 60.96 cm)

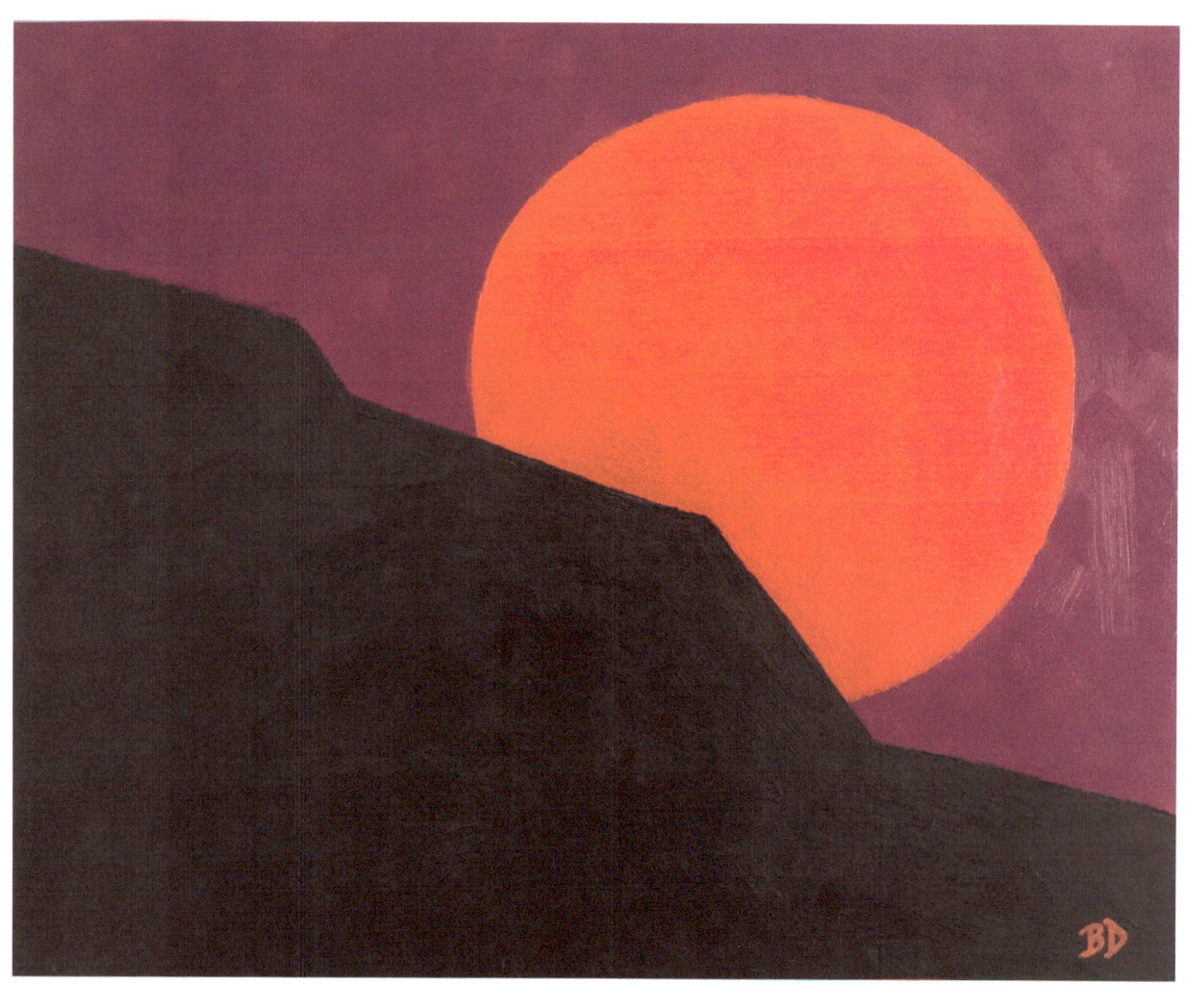

Purple Mountain, Red Sun
2020, Acrylic on Wood Panel, 16 x 20 inches (40.64 x 50.8 cm)

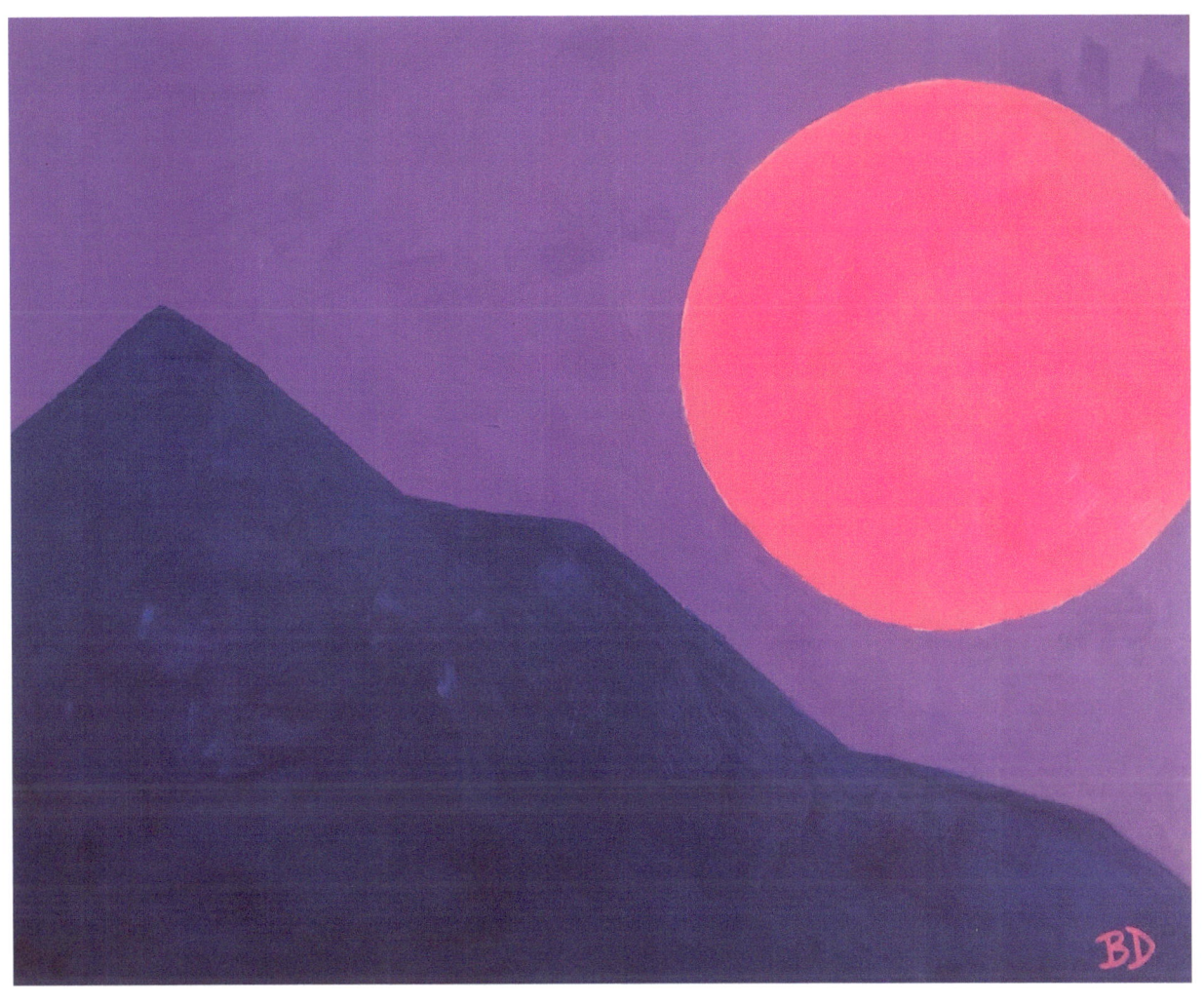

Purple Mountain, Pink Moon
2020, Acrylic on Wood Panel, 16 x 20 inches (40.64 x 50.8 cm)

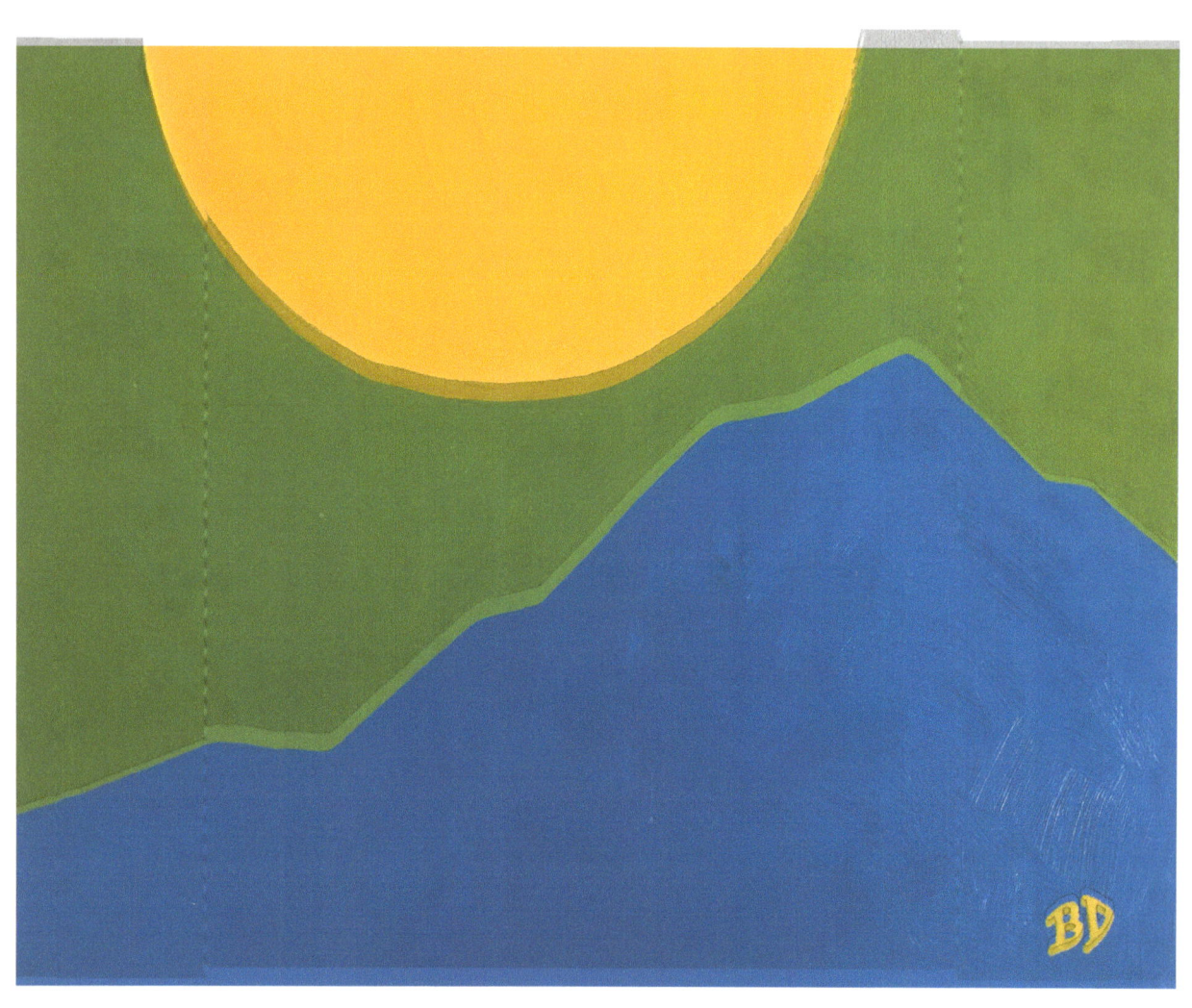

Blue Mountain, Yellow Sun
2020, Acrylic on Wood Panel, 11 x 14 inches (27.94 x 35.56 cm)

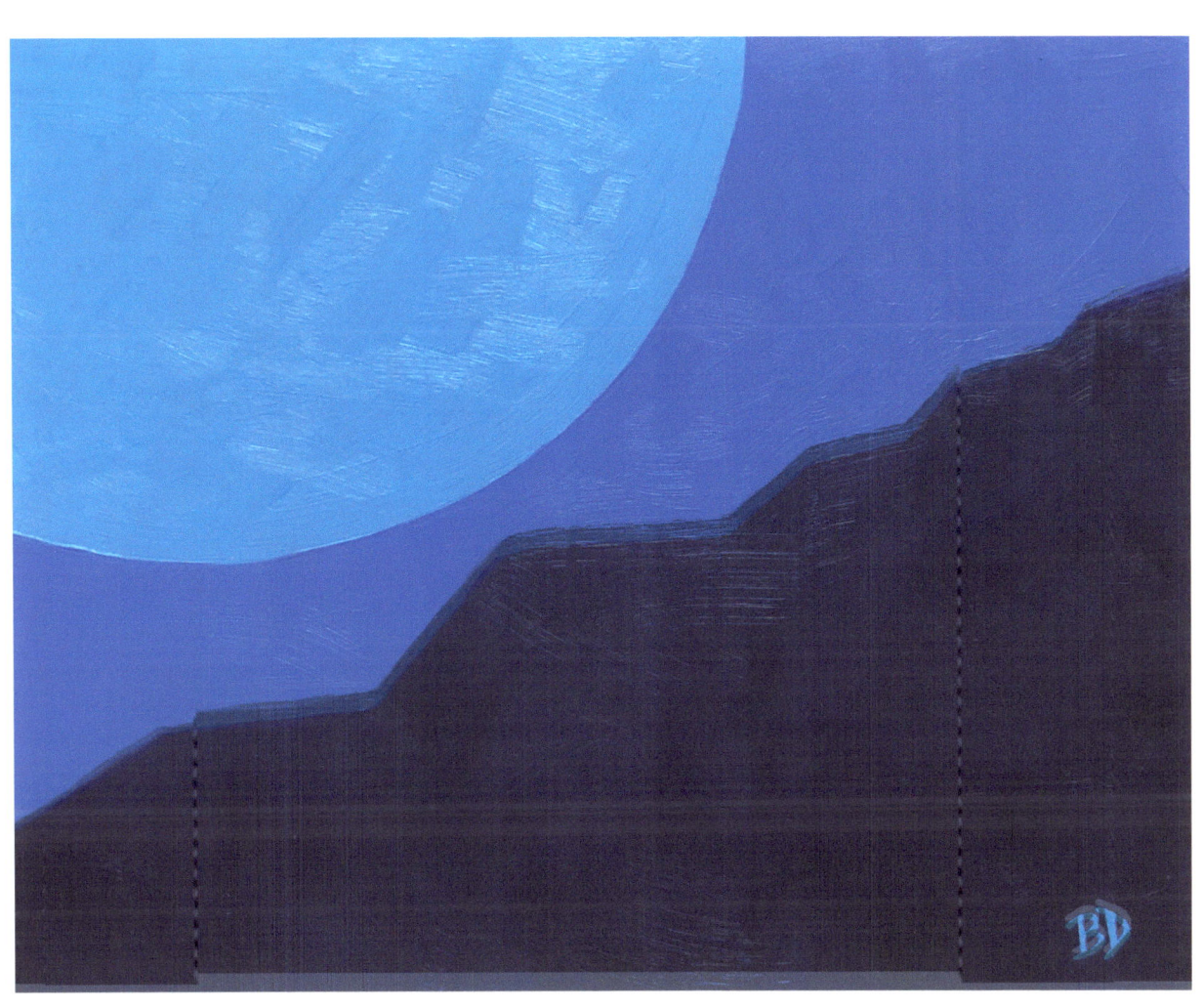

Blue Mountain, Blue Moon
2020, Acrylic on Wood Panel, 11 x 14 inches (27.94 x 35.56 cm)

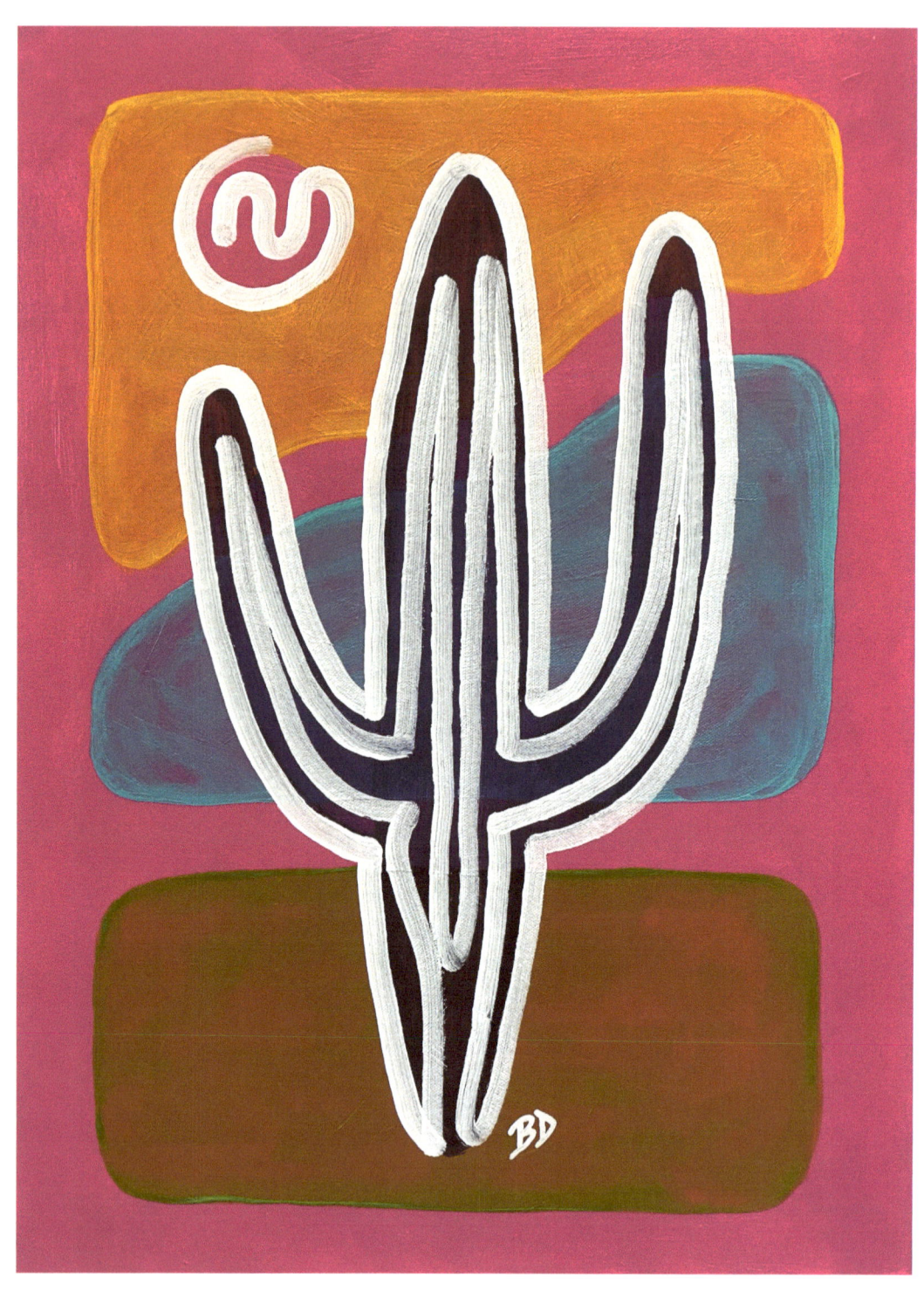

White Saguaro
2020, Acrylic on Canvas, 18 x 24 inches (45.72 x 60.96 cm)

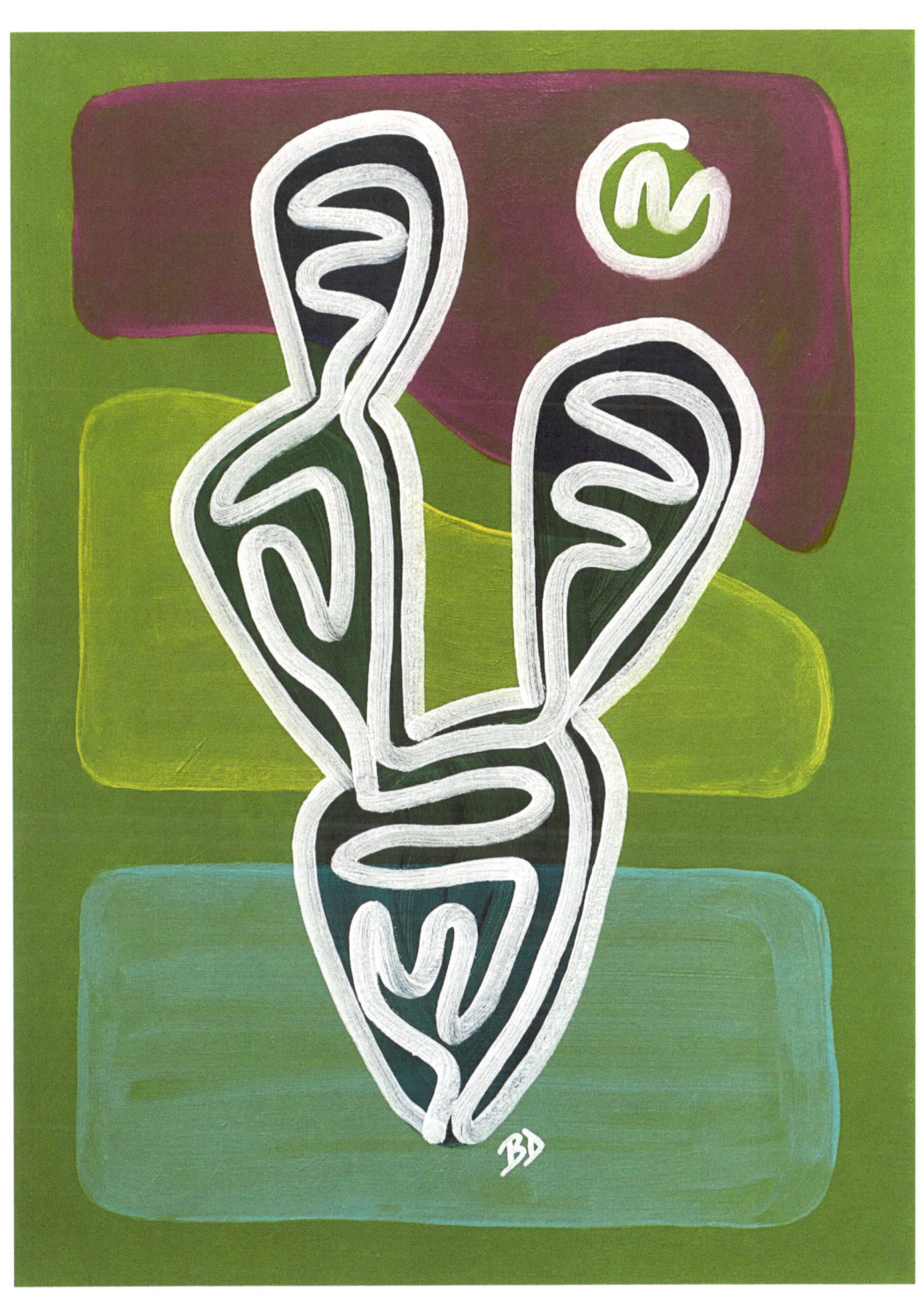

White Prickly Pear
2020, Acrylic on Canvas, 18 x 24 inches (45.72 x 60.96 cm)

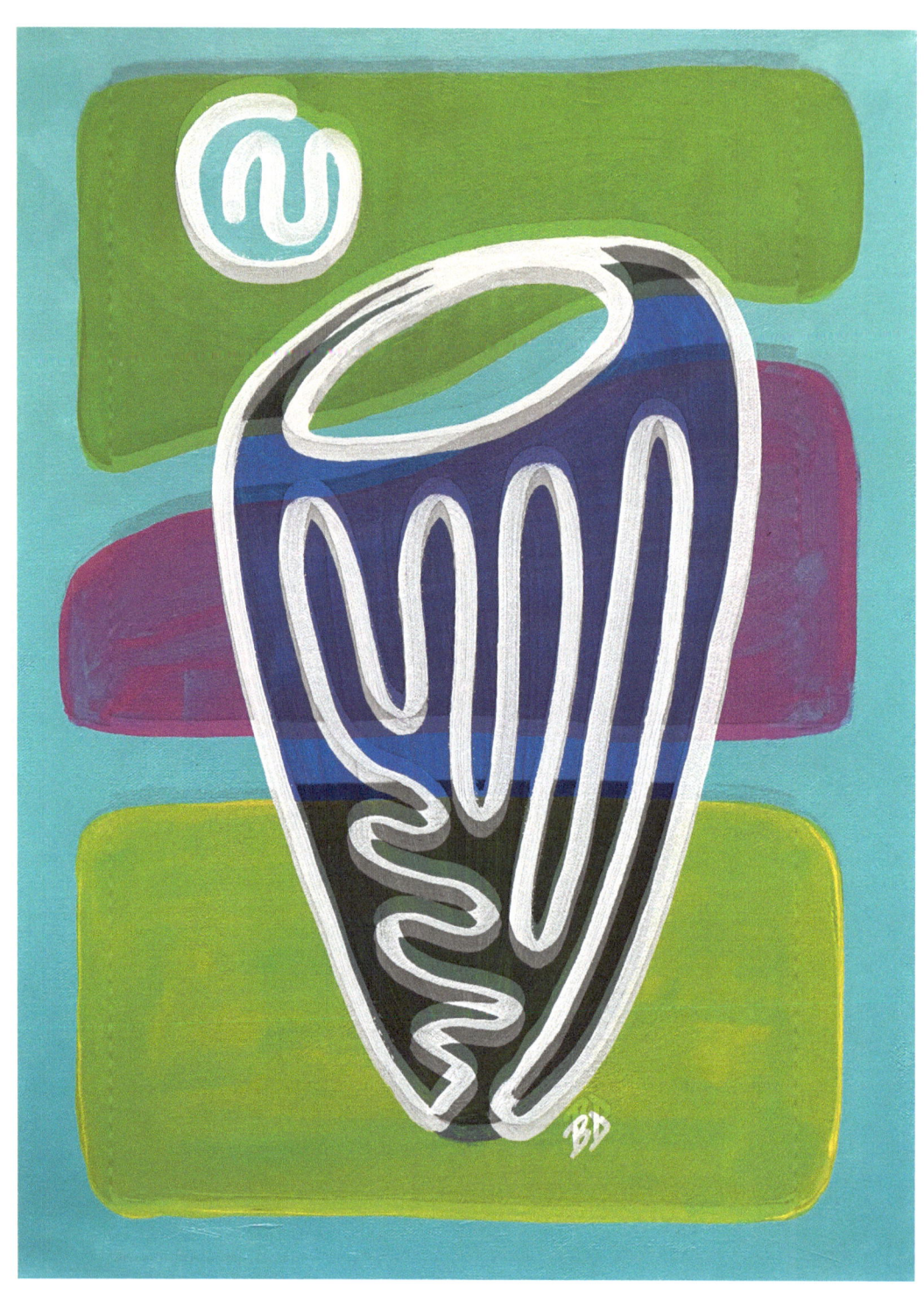

White Barrel Cactus
2020, Acrylic on Canvas, 18 x 24 inches (45.72 x 60.96 cm)

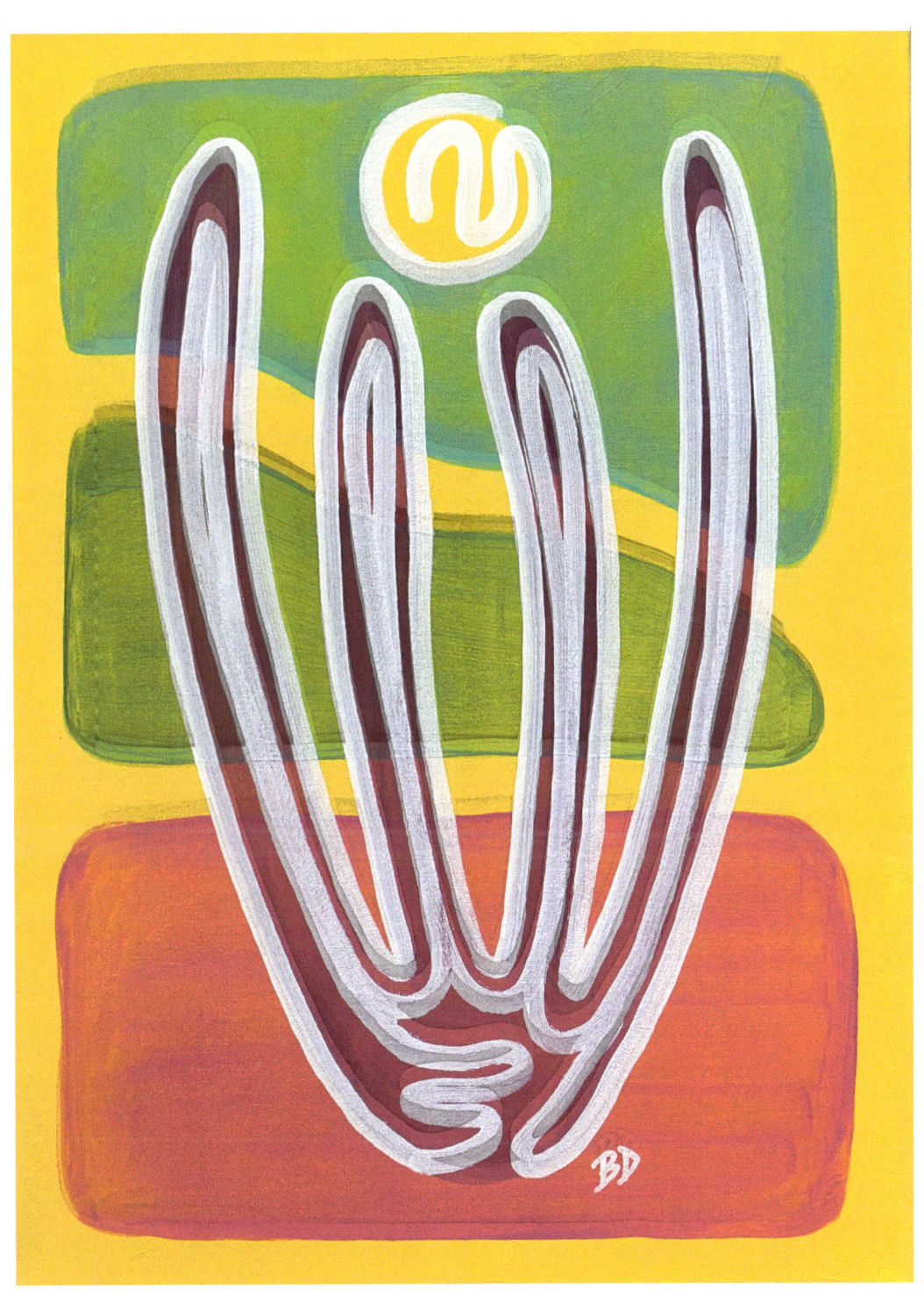

White Organ Pipe
2020, Acrylic on Canvas, 18 x 24 inches (45.72 x 60.96 cm)

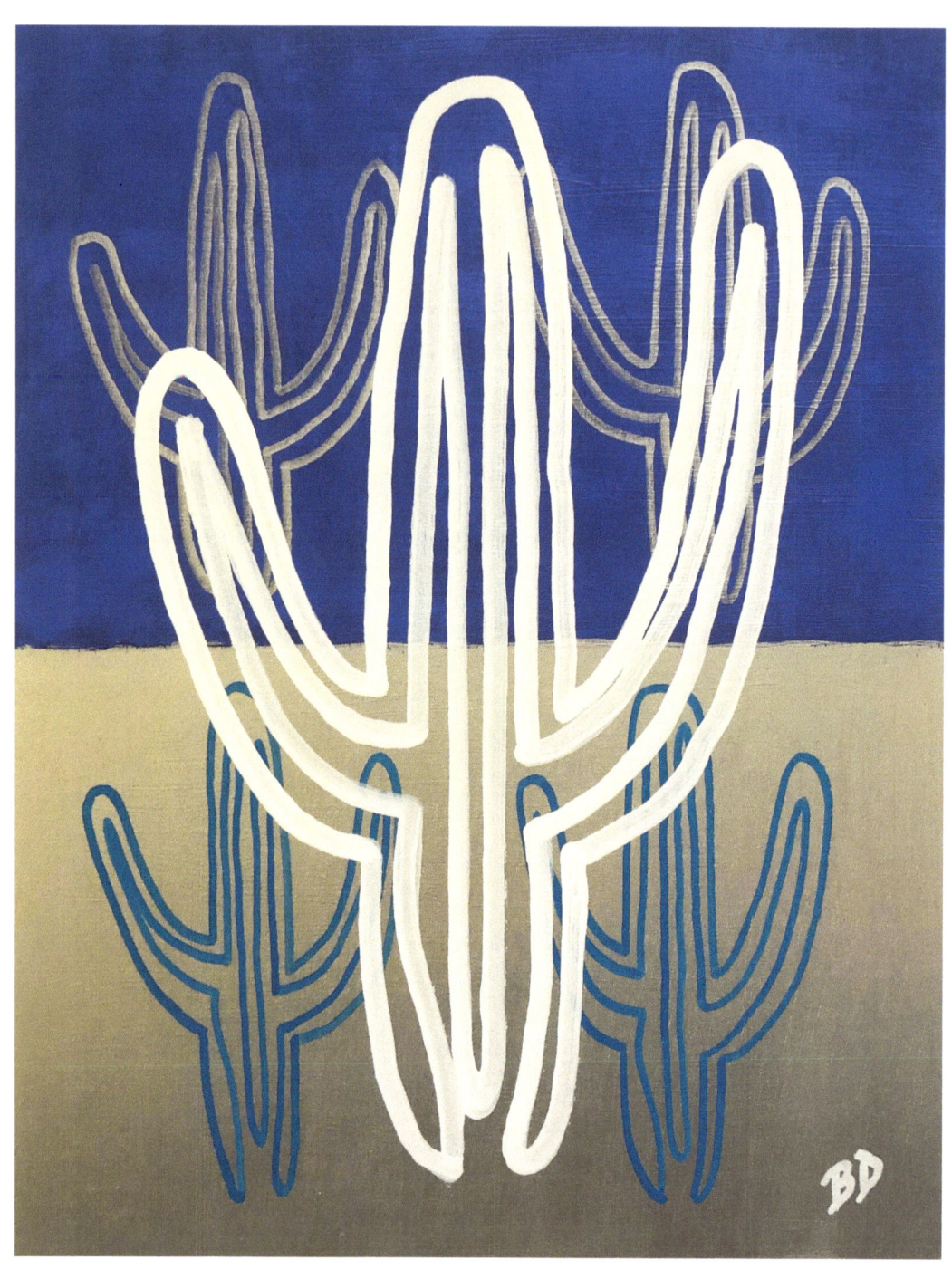

White Saguaro on Blue and Silver
2018, Acrylic on Wood Panel, 11 x 14 inches (27.94 x 35.56 cm)

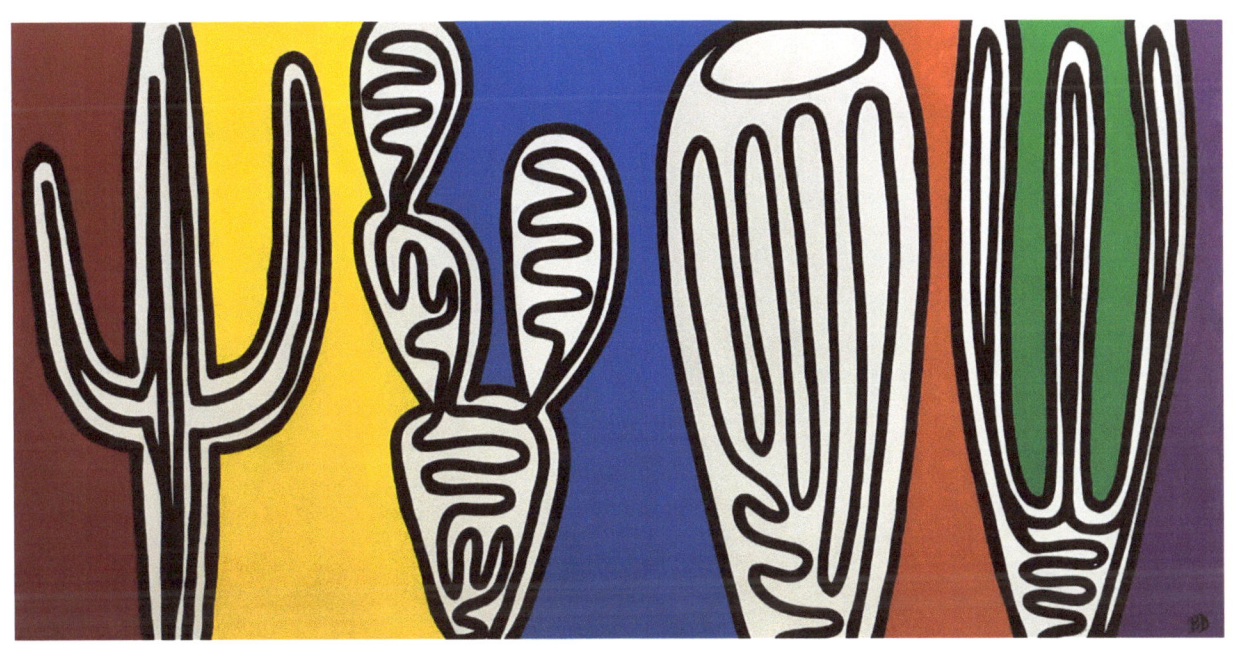

Four Cacti
2019, Acrylic on Canvas, 24 x 48 inches (60.96 x 121.92 cm)

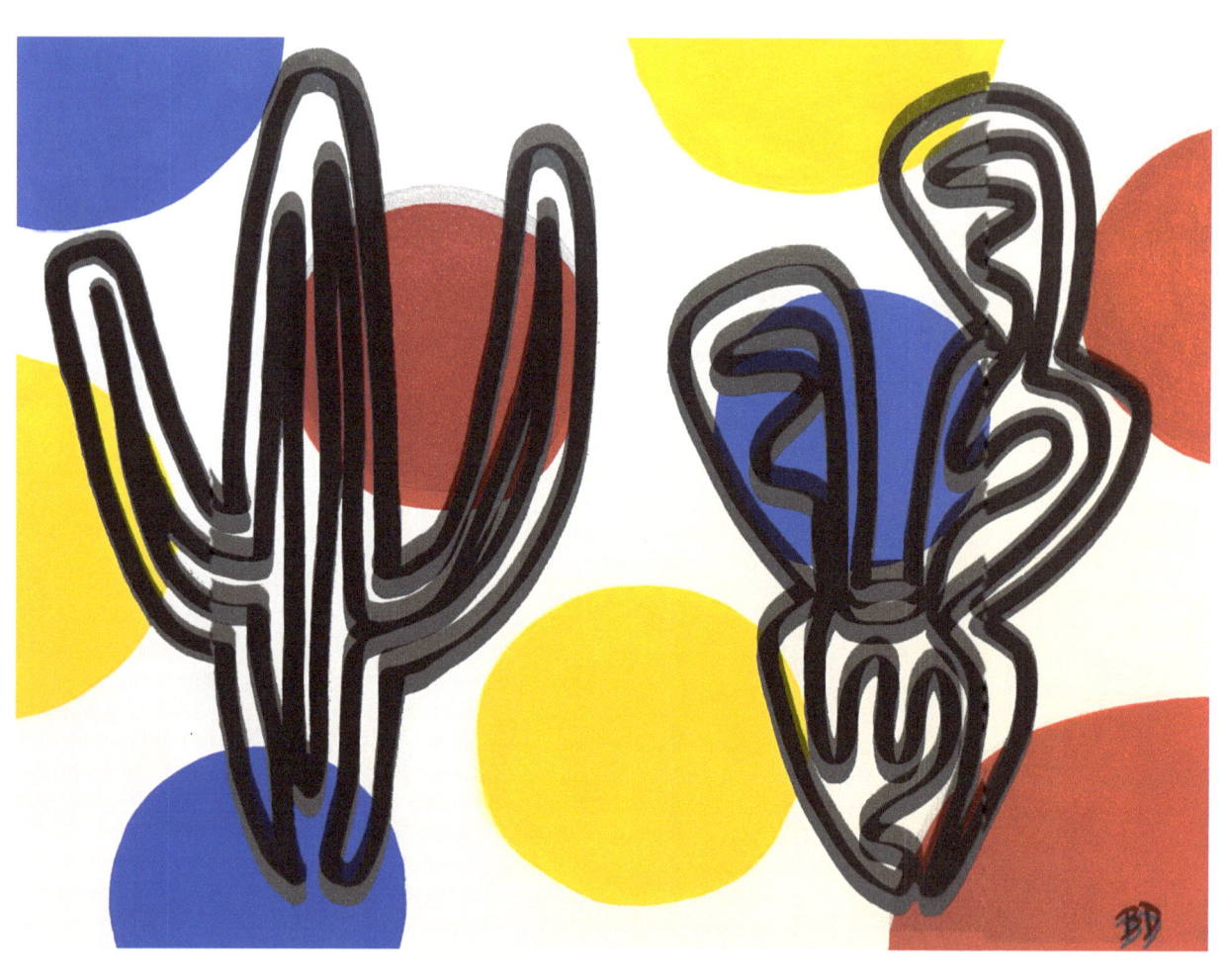

Saguaro and Prickly Pear on Primary Dots
2019, Acrylic on Canvas, 18 x 24 inches (45.72 x 60.96 cm)

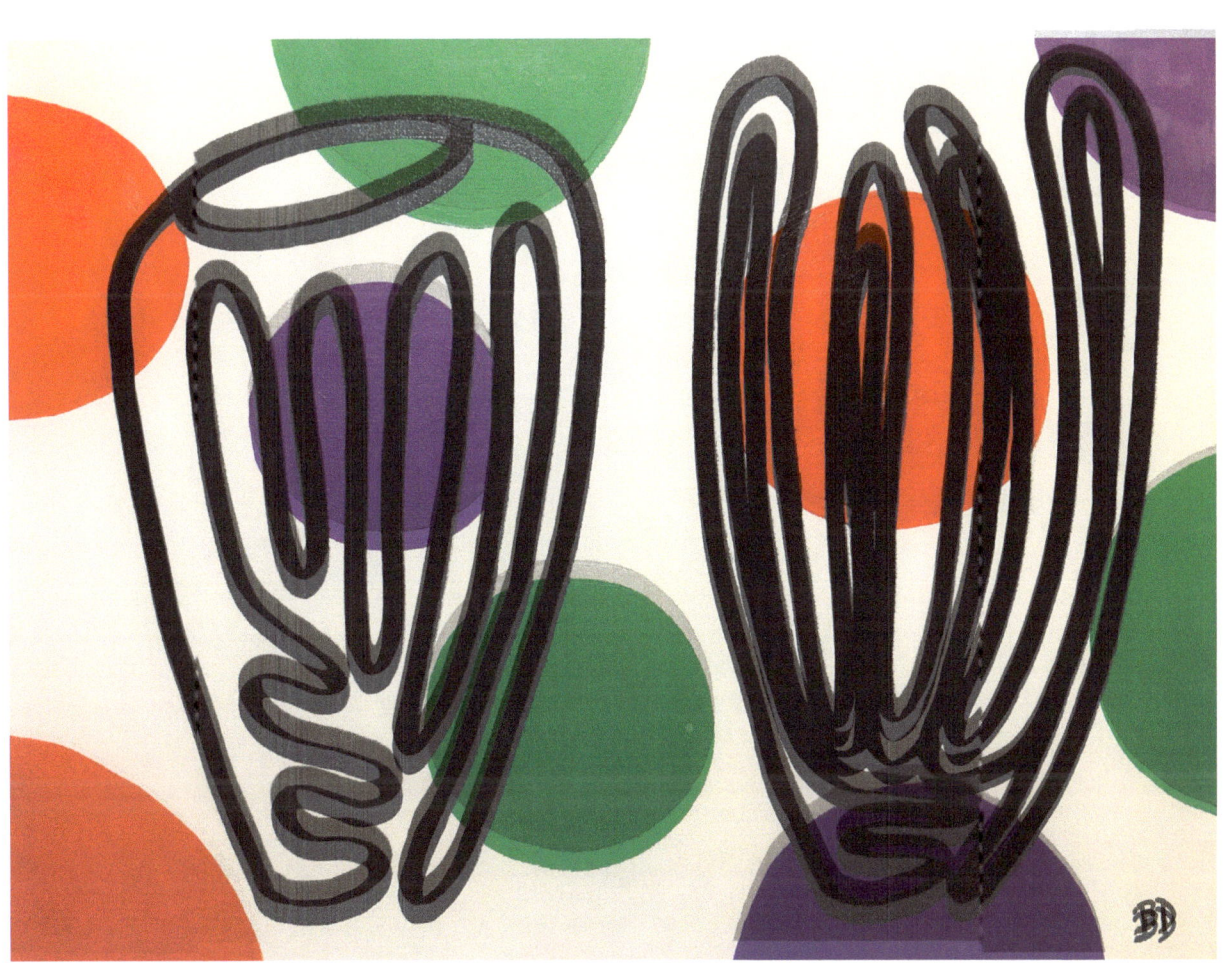

Barrel Cactus and Organ Pipe on Secondary Dots
2019, Acrylic on Canvas, 18 x 24 inches (45.72 x 60.96 cm)

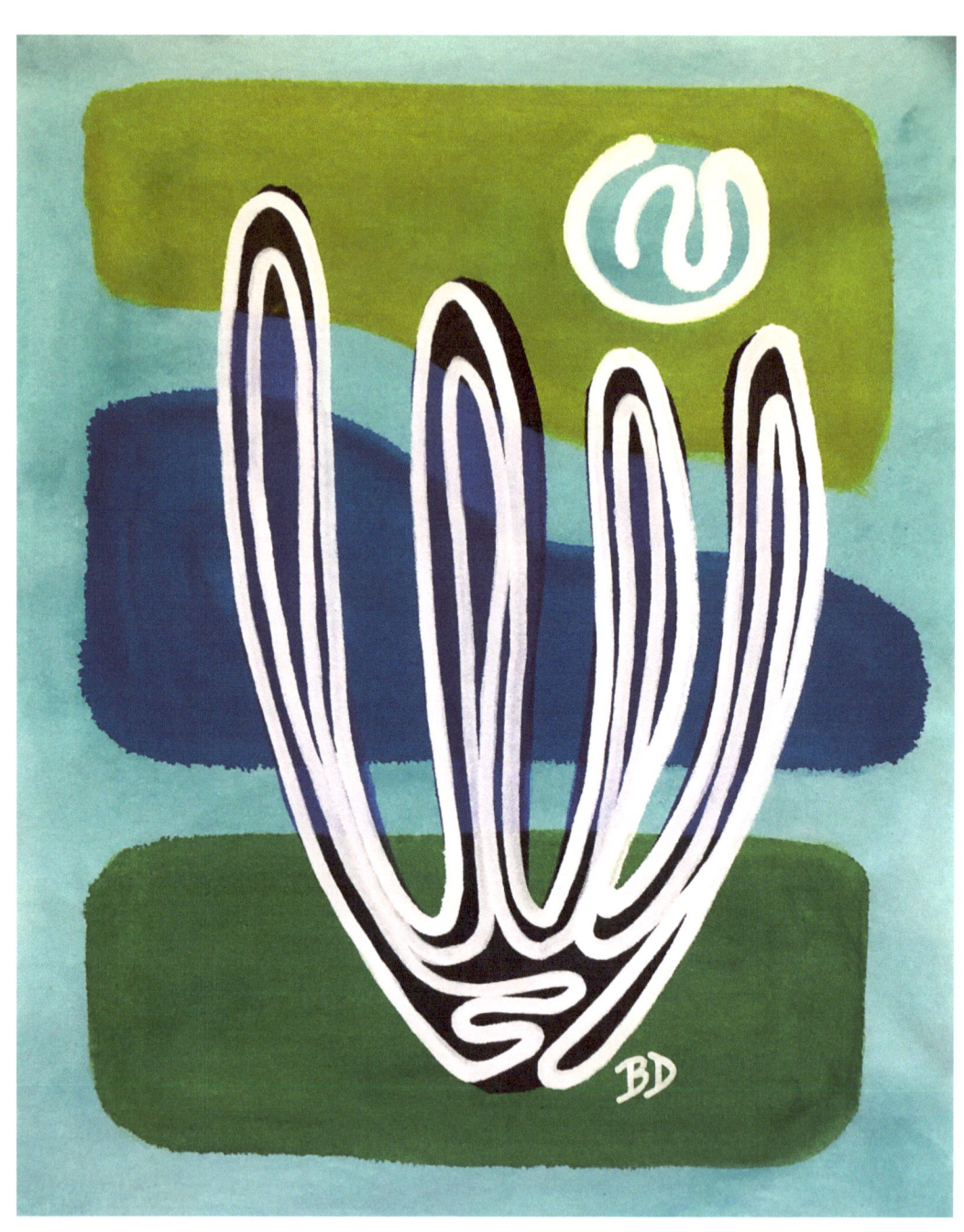

White Organ Pipe
2019, Acrylic Stain on Unprimed Canvas Mounted on Wood Panel, 16 x 20 inches (40.64 x 50.8 cm)

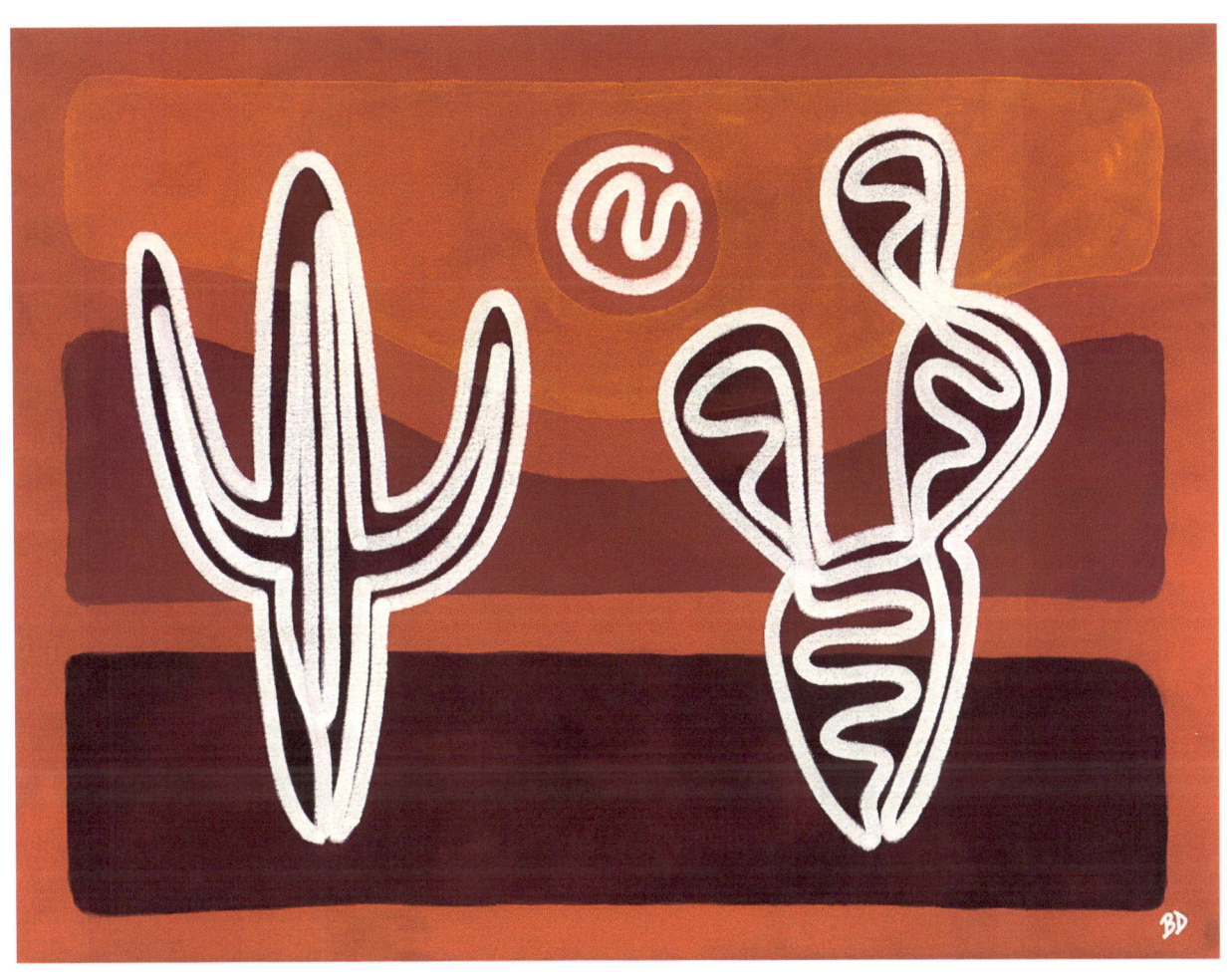

White Saguaro and Prickly Pear
2020, Acrylic Stain on Unprimed Canvas, 36 x 48 inches (91.44 cm x 121.92 cm)

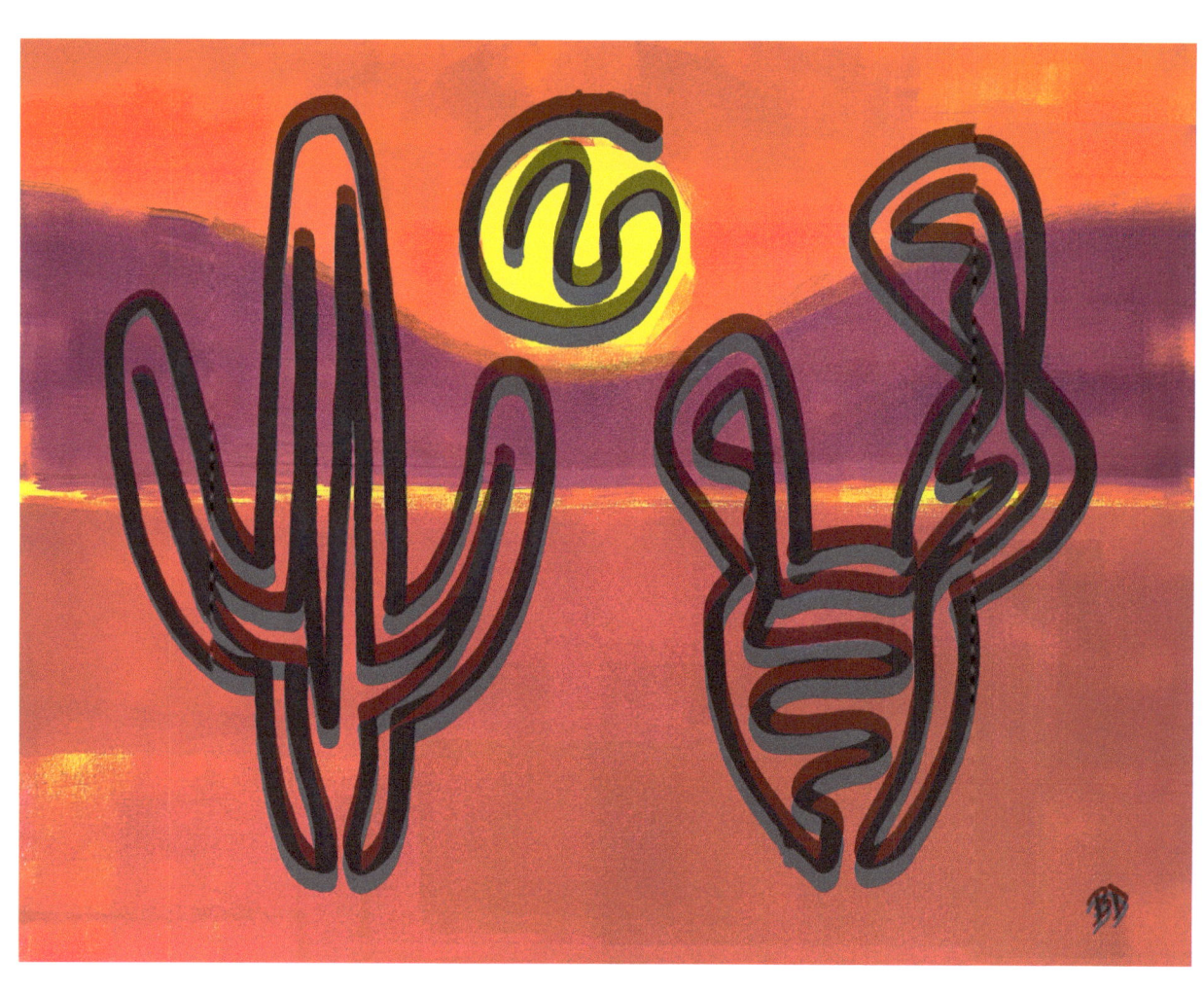

Black Saguaro and Prickly Pear
2020, Acrylic on Paper, 18 x 24 inches (45.72 x 60.96 cm)

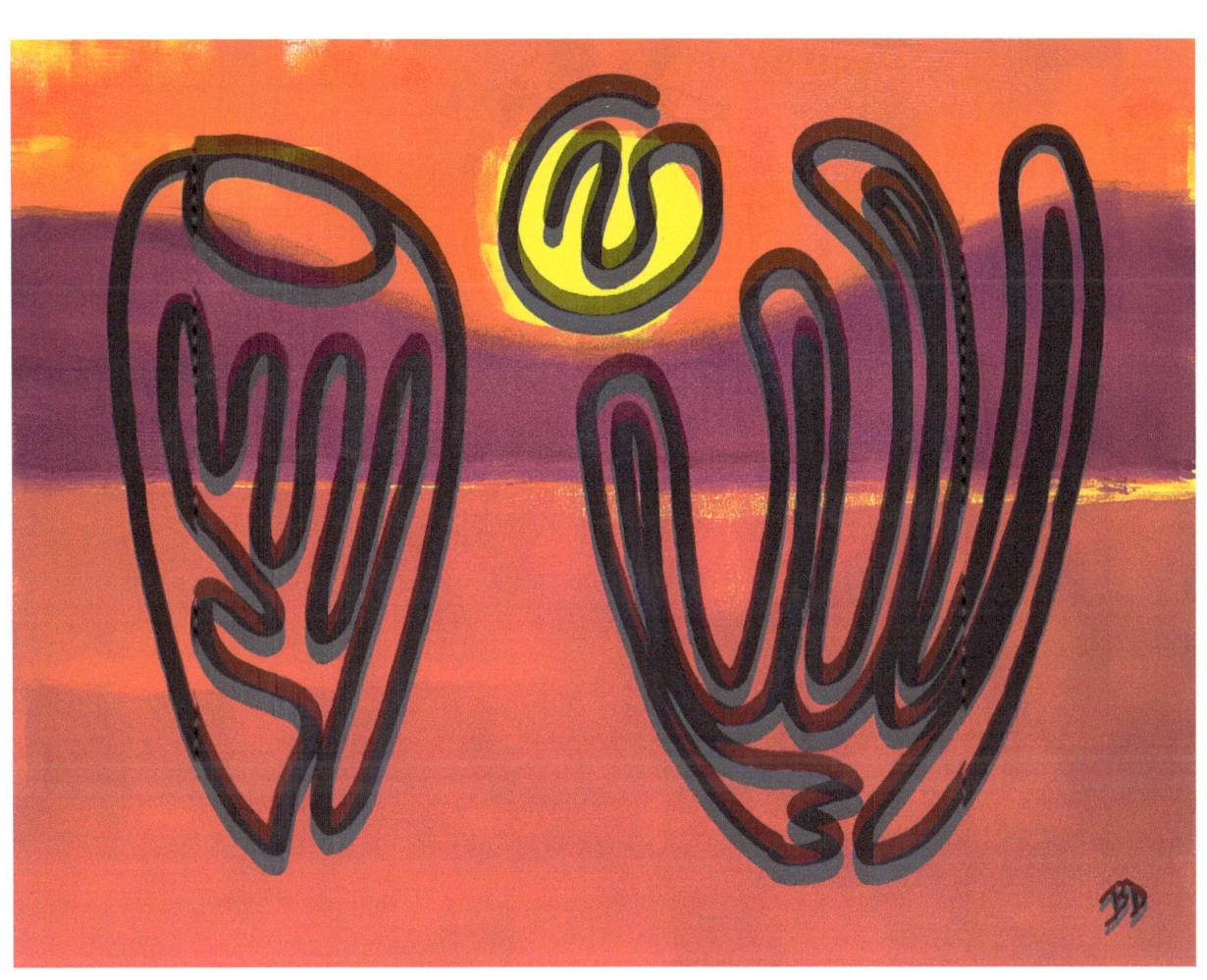

Black Barrel Cactus and Organ Pipe
2020, Acrylic on Paper, 18 x 24 inches (45.72 x 60.96 cm)

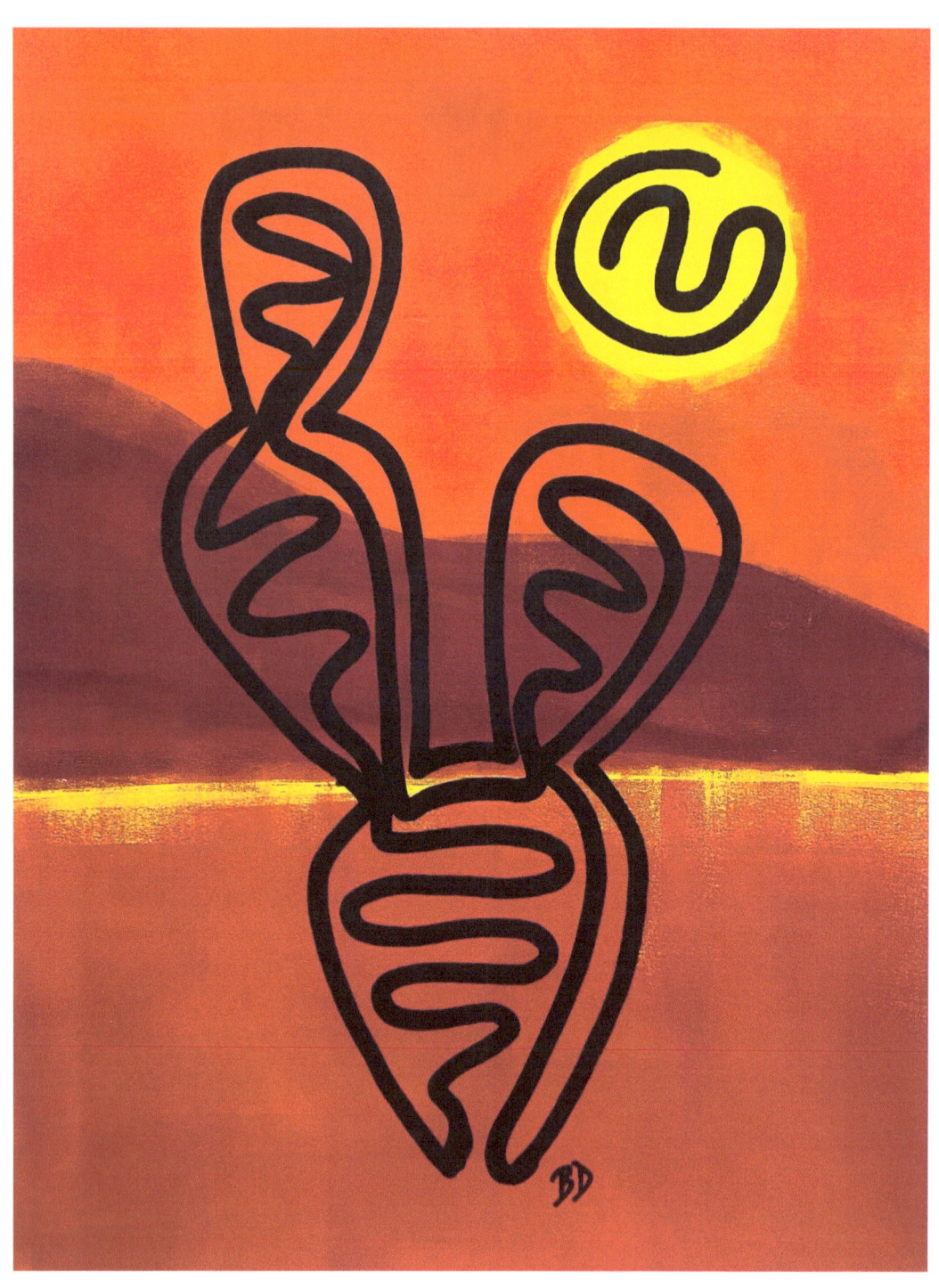

Black Prickly Pear
2020, Acrylic on Paper, 18 x 24 inches (45.72 x 60.96 cm)

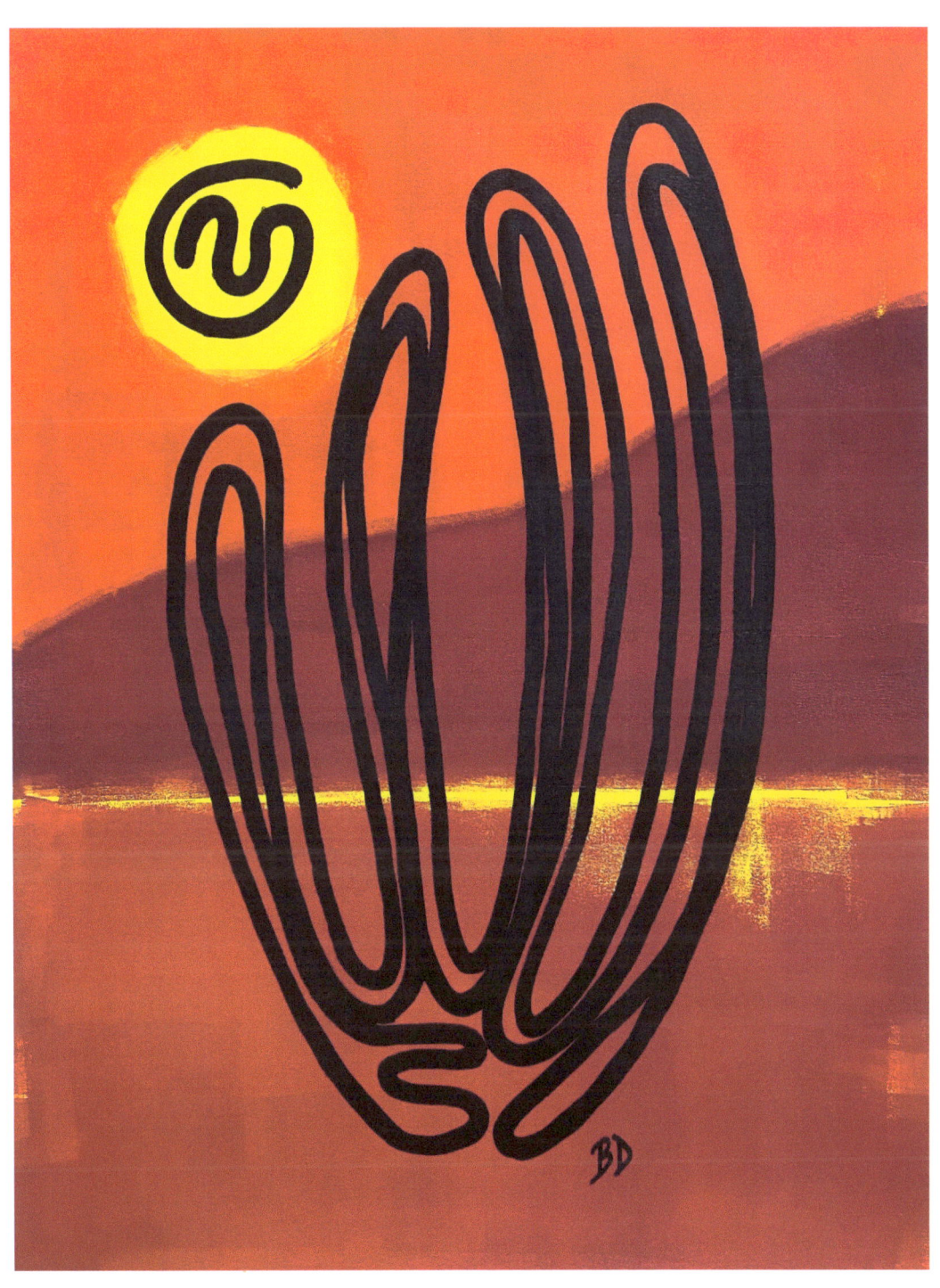

Black Organ Pipe
2020, Acrylic on Paper, 18 x 24 inches (45.72 x 60.96 cm)

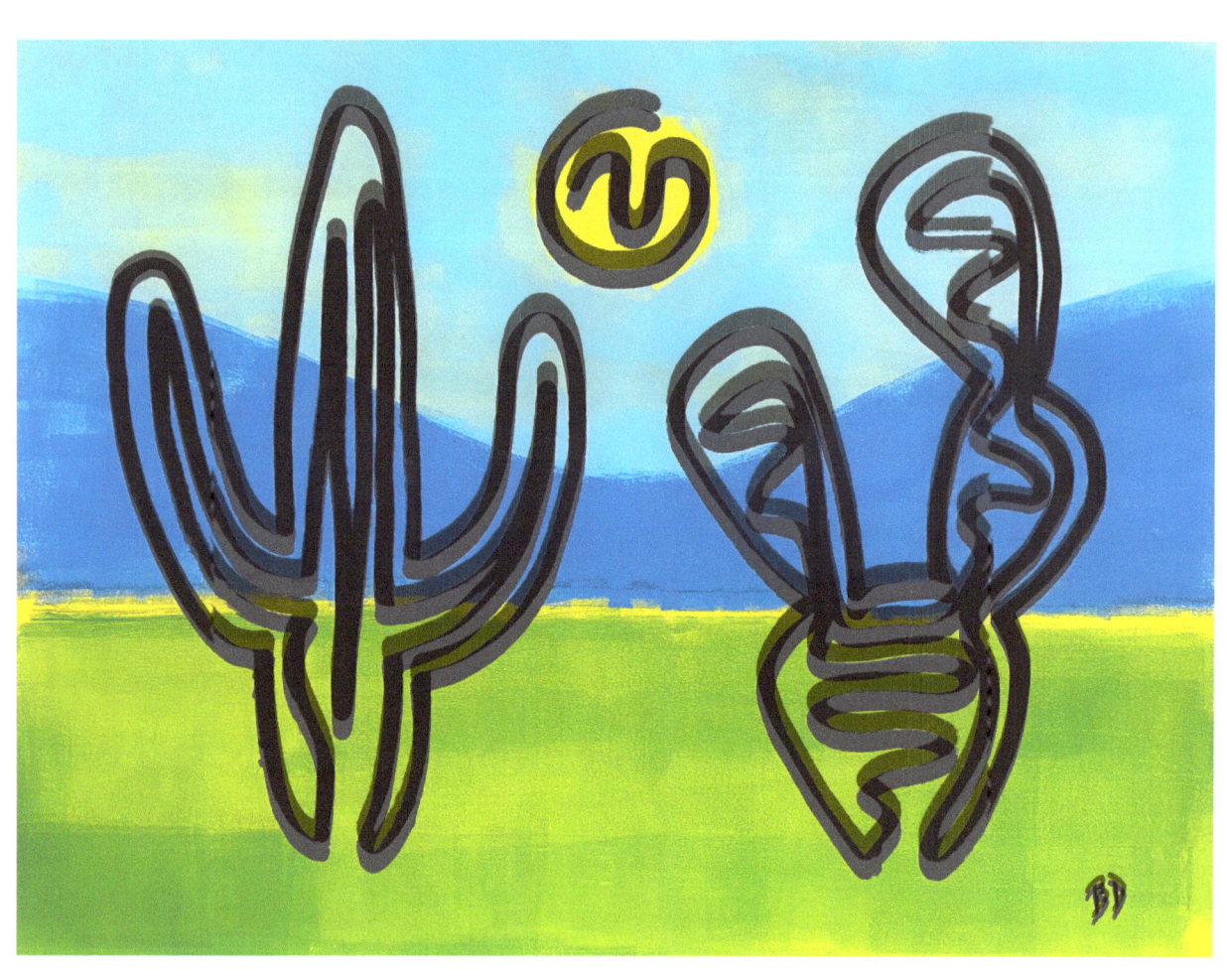

Black Saguaro and Prickly Pear
2020, Acrylic on Paper, 18 x 24 inches (45.72 x 60.96 cm)

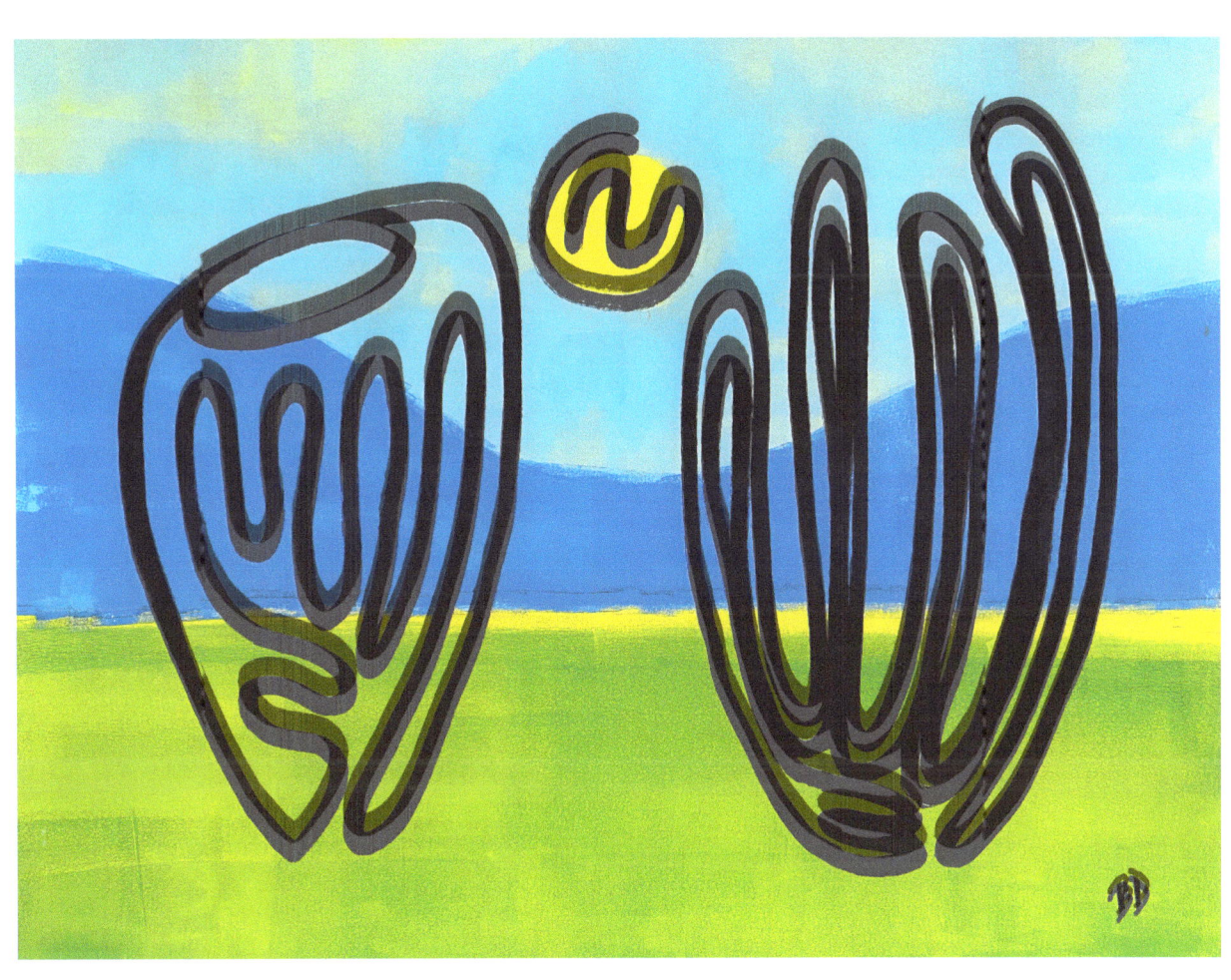

Black Barrel Cactus and Organ Pipe
2020, Acrylic on Paper, 18 x 24 inches (45.72 x 60.96 cm)

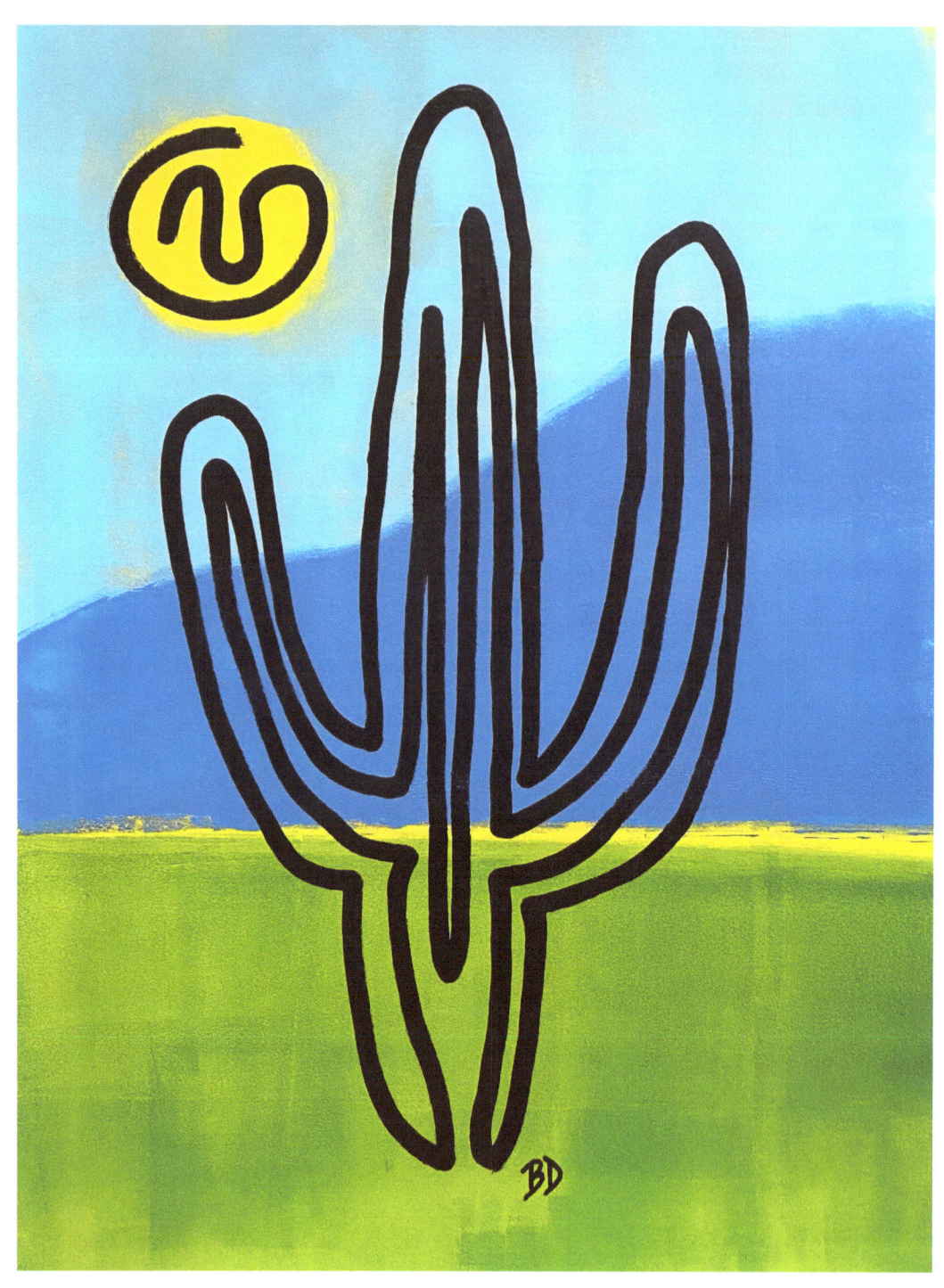

Black Saguaro
2020, Acrylic on Paper, 18 x 24 inches (45.72 x 60.96 cm)

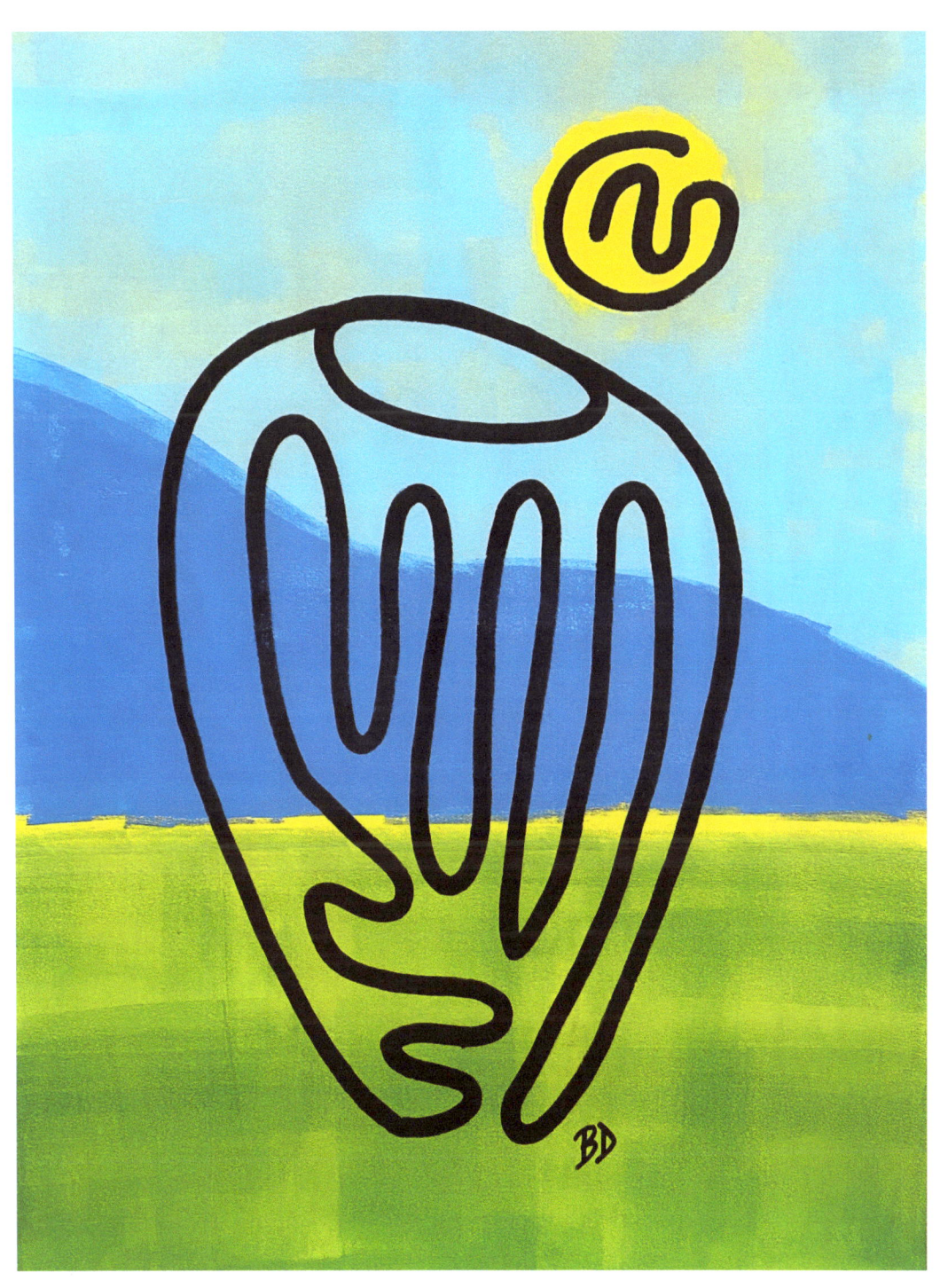

Black Barrel Cactus
2020, Acrylic on Paper, 18 x 24 inches (45.72 x 60.96 cm)

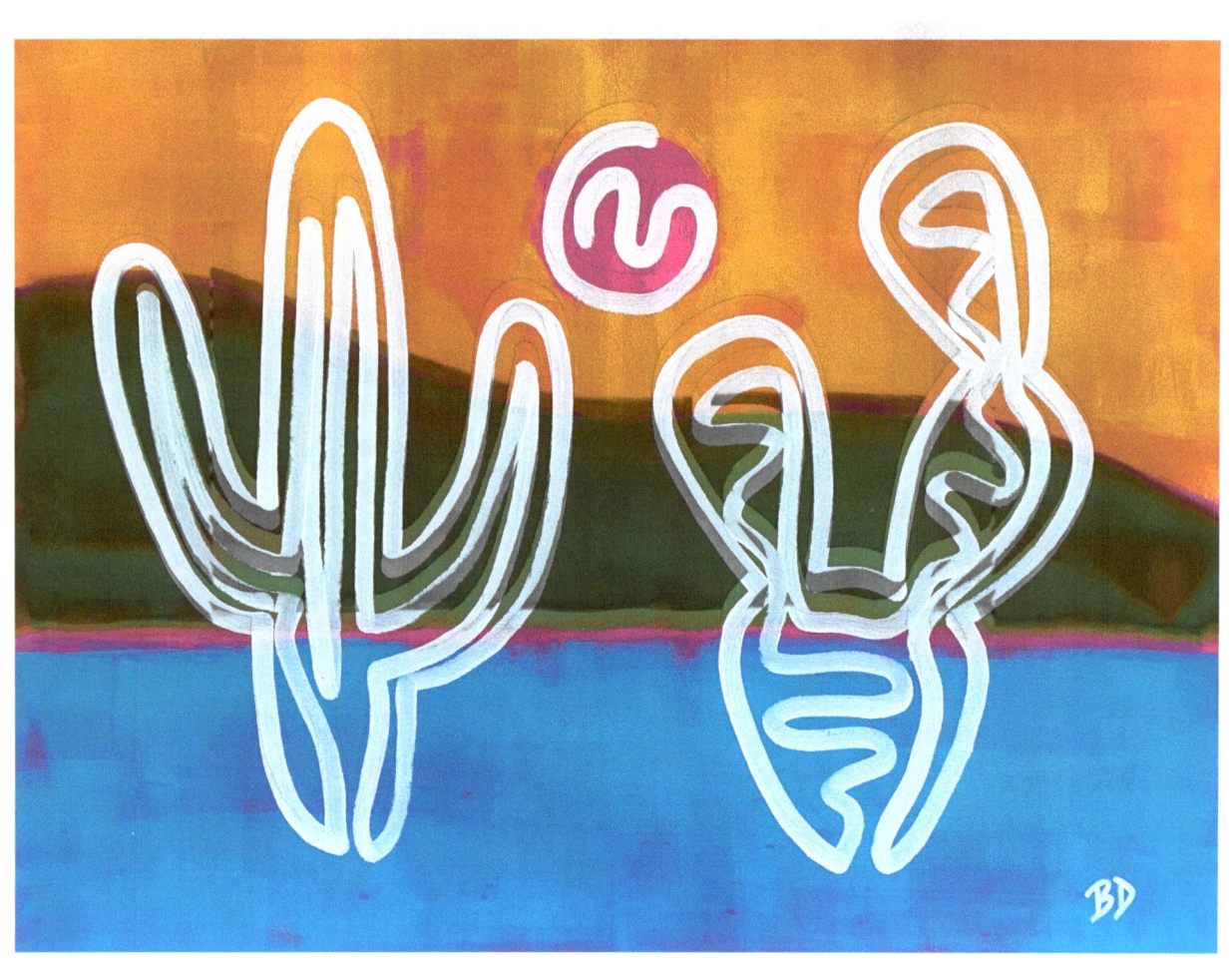

White Saguaro and Prickly Pear
2020, Acrylic on Paper, 18 x 24 inches (45.72 x 60.96 cm)

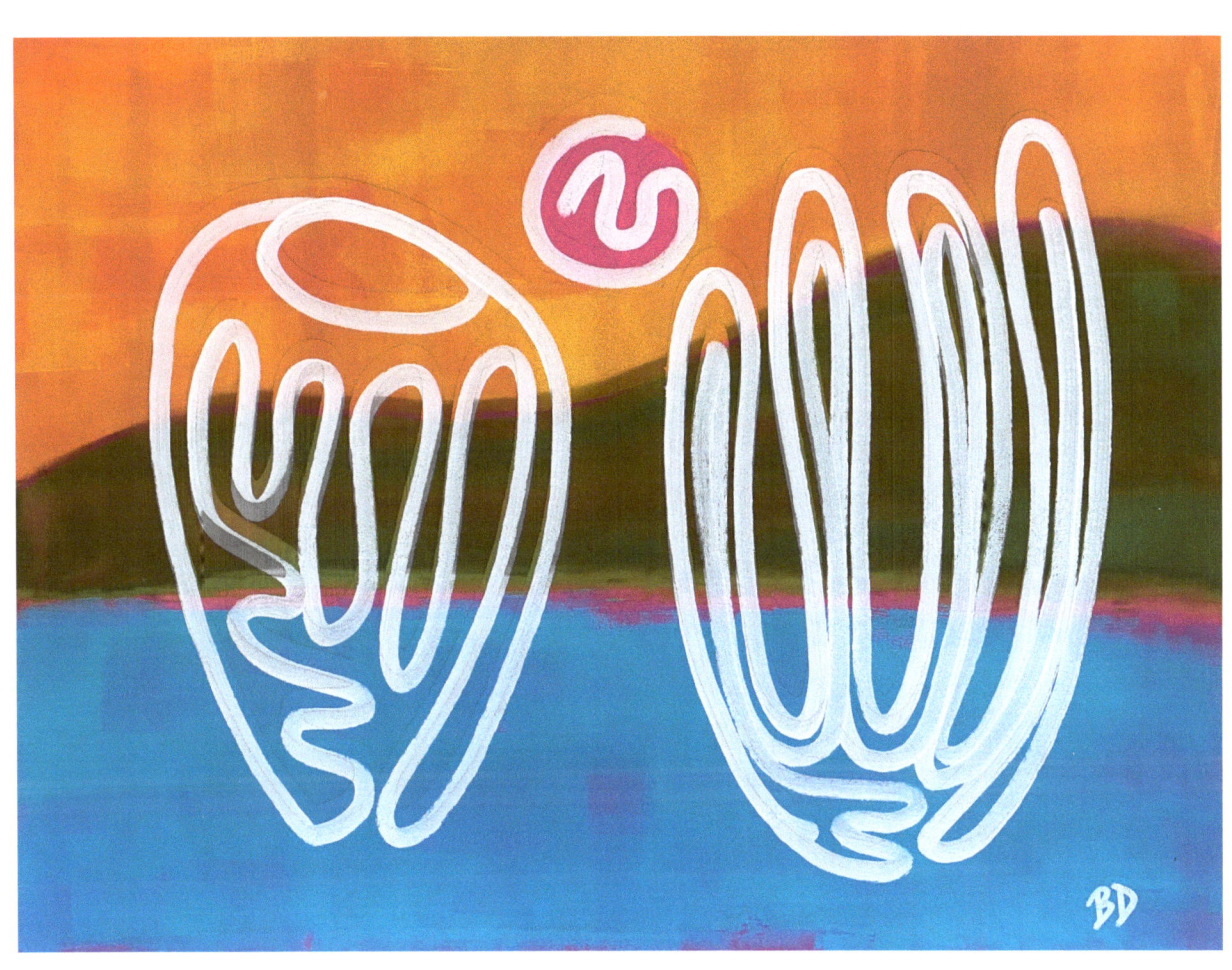

White Barrel Cactus and Organ Pipe
2020, Acrylic on Paper, 18 x 24 inches (45.72 x 60.96 cm)

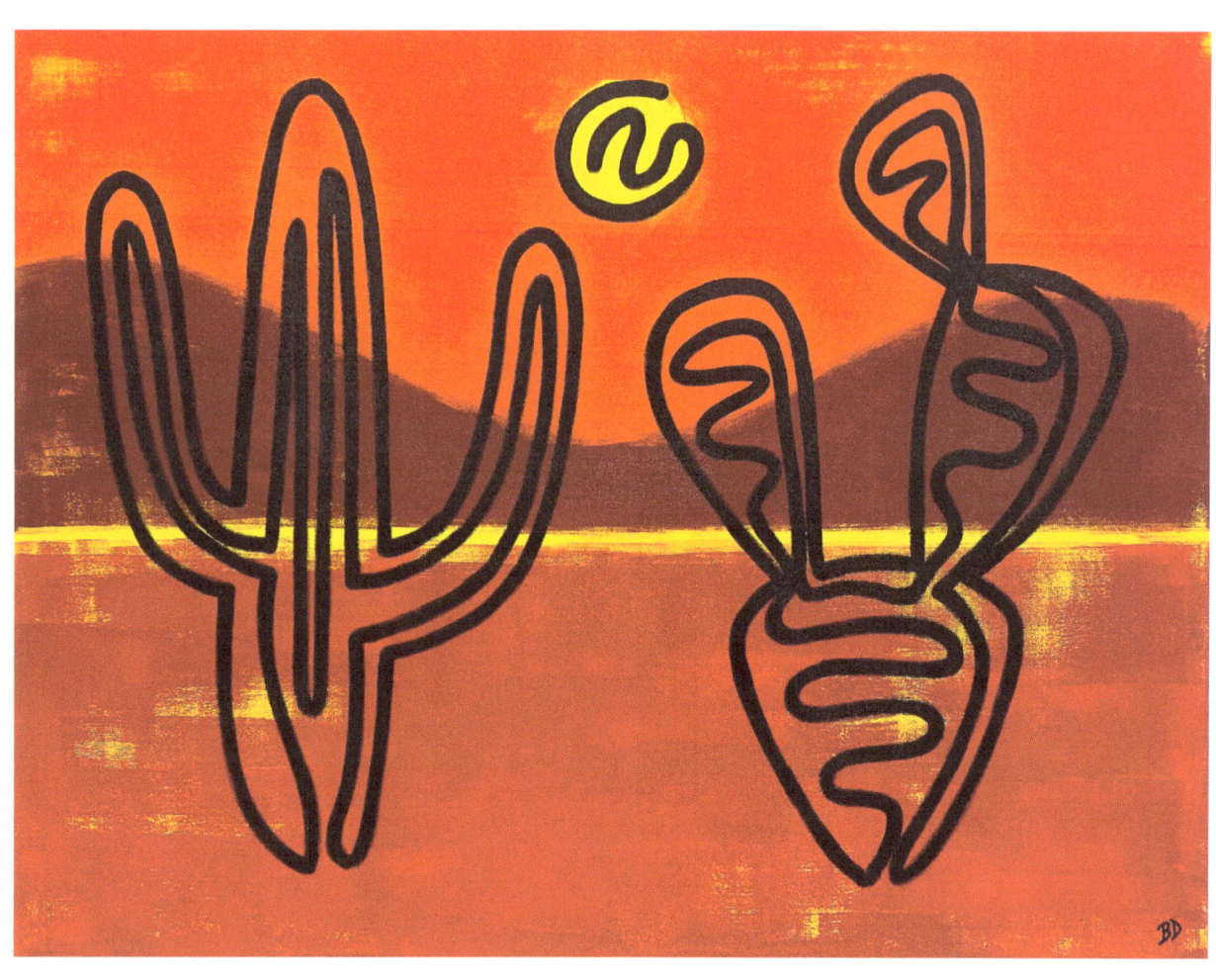

Black Saguaro and Prickly Pear
2020, Acrylic on Canvas, 36 x 48 inches (91.44 cm x 121.92 cm)

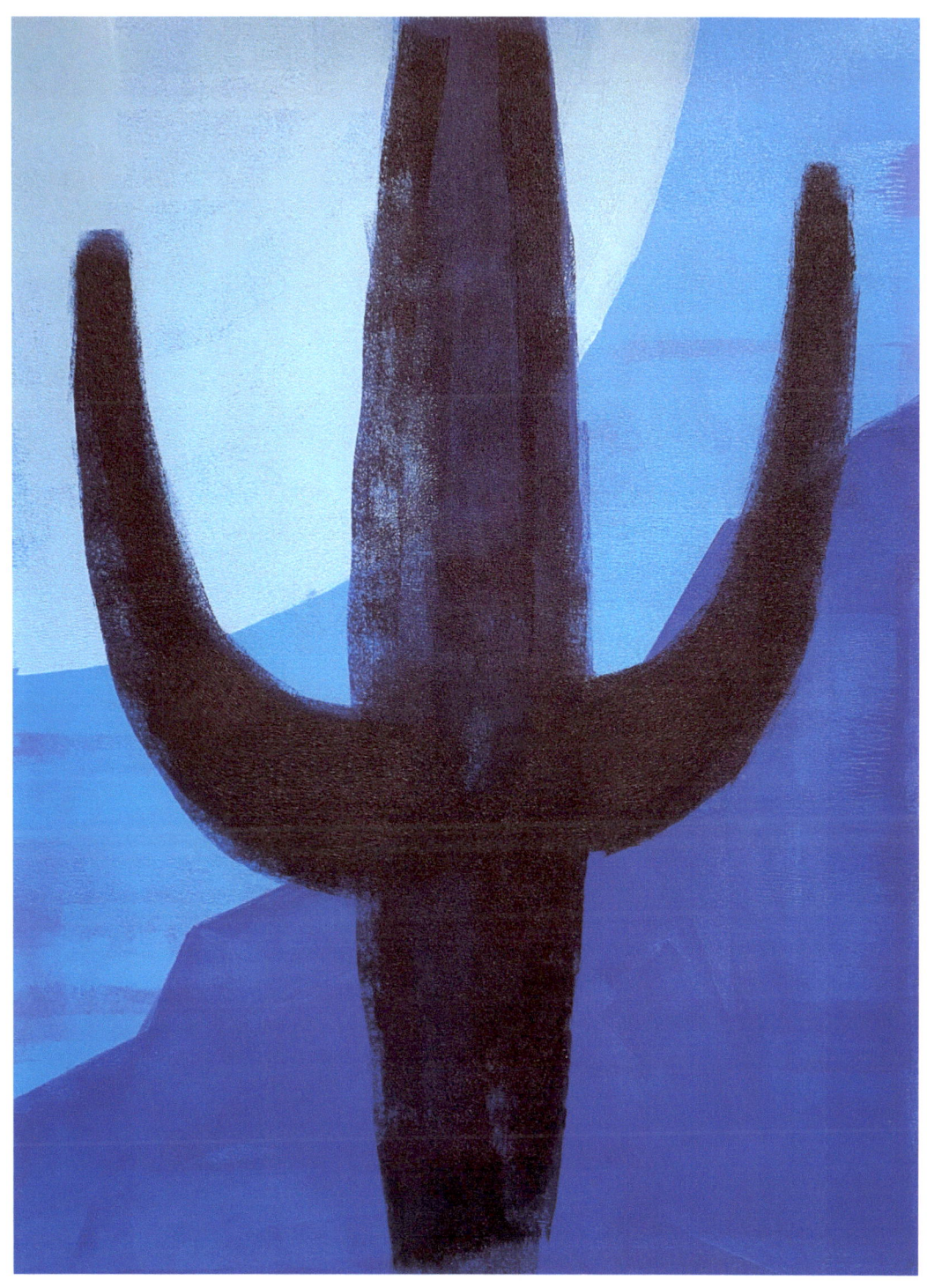

Blue Saguaro
2020, Acrylic on Paper, 18 x 24 inches (45.72 x 60.96 cm)

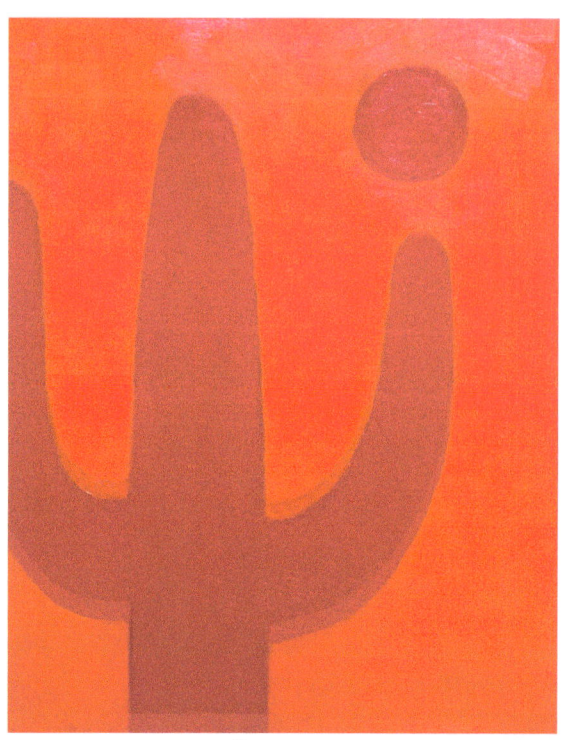

Saguaro
2019, Acrylic on Wood Panel, 8 x 10 inches (20.32 x 25.4 cm)

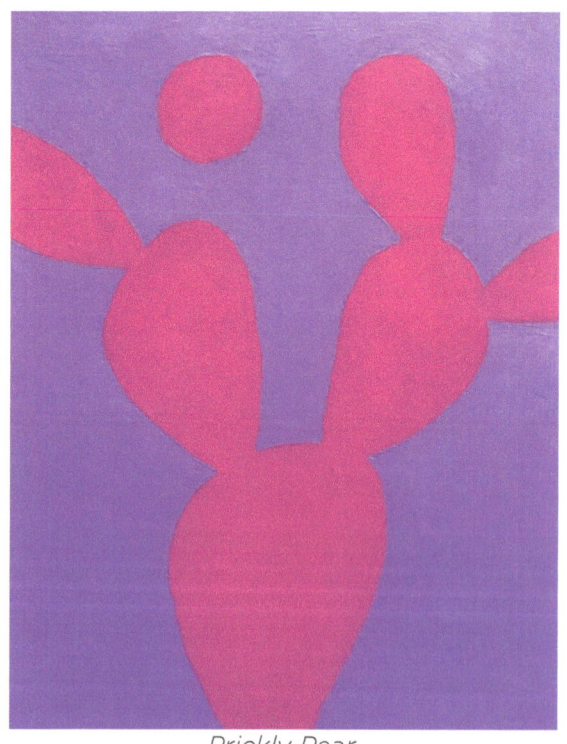

Prickly Pear
2019, Acrylic on Wood Panel, 8 x 10 inches (20.32 x 25.4 cm)

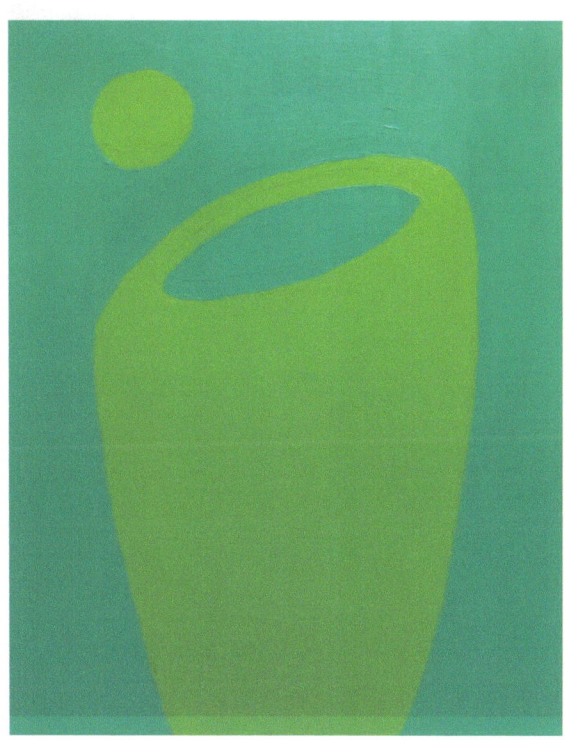

Barrel Cactus
2019, Acrylic on Wood Panel, 8 x 10 inches (20.32 x 25.4 cm)

Organ Pipe
2019, Acrylic on Wood Panel, 8 x 10 inches (20.32 x 25.4 cm)

See more of my work at

bdabstracts.com

For merchandise see

cactusvibe.com

My other landscape work can be found at

rjdfineart.com

www.ingramcontent.com/pod-product-compliance
Lightning Source LLC
Chambersburg PA
CBHW051919210526
45473CB00006B/2065